The

WISDOM OF ANGELS

UNEARTHING MY ITALIAN ROOTS

by

MARTHA T. CUMMINGS

IN OCTOBER NOON

BEST WISHES / TANTI AUGURI!

BRANDEN BOOKS, INC.
P.O. BOX 812094
Wellesley, MA 02482

BOSTON

Library of Congress Cataloging-in-Publication Data

Cummings, Matha T.
Wisdom of angels : unearthing my Italian roots / by Martha T. Cummings

ISBN 0-8283-2072-1 (alk. Paper)
1. Italy—Description and travel.
2. Cummings, Martha T.—Journeys—Italy
3. Cummings, Martha T.—Family. I Title.
DG430.2 .C854 2002
914.504'84—dc21 2002002250

BRANDEN BOOKS
Division of Branden Publishing Company
PO Box 812094
Wellesley, MA 02482

CONTENTS

Dedication			5
Preface			7
Map of Italy			8
Chapter 1	Bridges	Gli Stati Uniti/Italia	9
Chapter 2	Dances	Campo di Giove, Abruzzo	22
Chapter 3	Magic	Campo di Giove, Abruzzo	42
Chapter 4	Angels	Campo di Giove, Abruzzo	68
	Family Tree	Campo di Giove, Abruzzo	86
Chapter 5	Wonders	Magliano dei Marsi, Abruzzo	87
Chapter 6	Boundaries	Firenze, Toscana	108
Chapter 7	Views	Pettineo, Sicilia	118
Chapter 8	Whispers	Tusa, Sicilia	131
Chapter 9	Truth	Tusa, Sicilia	153
	Family Tree	Tusa, Sicilia	163
Chapter 10	Deference	Palermo, Sicilia	164
Chapter 11	The Present	Italia/Gli Stati Uniti	190
The Epilogue			199
Acknowledgments			203
Photography Credits			206
About the Author			207

DEDICATION

For My Mother

Antoinette Frances Ragonese Cummings

…with much love, respect, and gratitude,
to my first angel.

PREFACE

There is an intensity of emotion that greets me in Italy when I visit the birthplaces of my mother's parents. The depth of the passion is often surprising despite the consistency of its arrival. And I welcome it, because it brings me back to the emotion of childhood – when we had been more likely to live viscerally and true to what we felt inside.

Returning to childhood in Italy spreads further, though, than raw emotion. It spreads to stories, smells, and touch that can get lost in the years and busyness of our lives. Grandparents' cheeks, voices, and laps return; parents appear tall, healthy, and strong; brothers, sisters, and cousins spend their minutes in bathing suits, playing tether ball, or taking family cookouts for granted.

I return to Italy to connect with a past that helped shape me…

but that runs the risk of being forgotten…

unless I keep it alive.

In writing as I do, then, some goals are simple – to encourage those who yearn to return to homeland to do exactly that, *any* of them, or *all* of them, so that they may: stand outside the places in which ancestors were born, meet the offspring of relatives who were left behind, and discover and uncover the documents, edifices, and genealogical tangents of their pasts, so that they may find and tell the truth, if their histories allow them such a privilege.

To those who have already been and have breathed, stared, and cried in ways that are different from what we do at home, I hope that *The Wisdom of Angels* will invigorate your memories and help you relive, again and again, how joyous a visit to childhood can be.

Grazie, e buon viaggio.

- Martha T. Cummings

UNA MAPPA D'ITALIA

The Wisdom of Angels is based on a trip in October, 1999.
This map indicates a rough approximation of the itinerary's sites.
A portion of the author's royalties will go to Alzheimer's research and care.

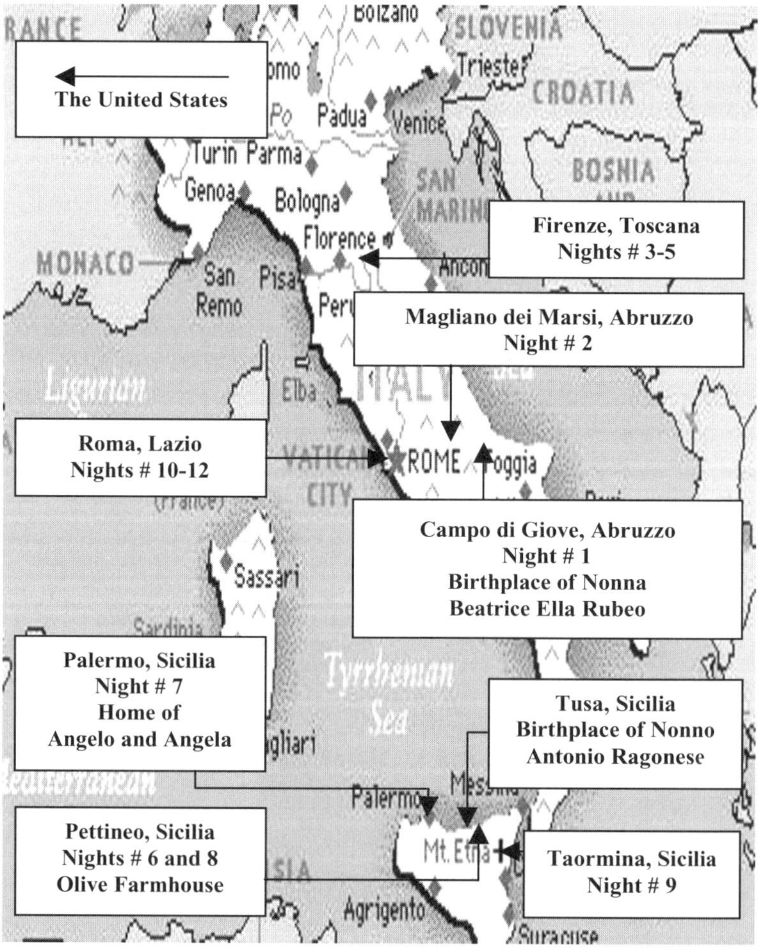

Chapter One

BRIDGES

Gli Stati Uniti/Italia

Italy.

Italia.

If I were able to reach it by bridge, I would live there.

I would live under the arches of copper-colored roofs and grape trellises. I would plant the kinds of tomatoes I dream about back home and fill my bathrooms with brightly-painted ceramic sinks from Santo Stéfano di Camastra. I would say *bo* at exactly the right moments and learn to seesaw with the linguistic rhythms, make my own wine, buy fresh bread, and visit Caravaggio and Modigliani as if they were old friends. And I would drive back and forth, from my new country to my old country, with wild abandon, and whenever the feeling moved me.

"Why don't they build a bridge?", I ask when I put the finishing touches on autumn plane reservations. Build a bridge from Boston to Rome, and help me avoid the searing reality of 300 over-packed and over-stimulated tourists sweeping over the clouds in a vacuum-sealed bus. Build a bridge, and allow me to drive to Italy. Let me snap on a life-jacket and the kind of seatbelt that might actually save me. Let me fill up my car with gas and lay my aeronautical neuroses to rest. Let me put in some *musica italiana*, turn up the volume, and head onto the bridge with a light heart, enough leg room, and no one pointing out the emergency exits.

Build a bridge.

Ma nessuno mi sente.

Instead, I make a plane reservation, stow my belongings as directed, and wish that I were as much enamored of parts I could find back home as I am of Italy. But I am not. So I have to prepare for takeoff, insert ear plugs, and feign glee in response to the flight attendant's offer of beverages and six peanuts in a bag. I never sleep, almost never get up, and mantra myself to exhaustion.

Turbulence is merely a bump in the road.

Turbulence is merely a bump in the road.

Except there is no road.

I remove my ear plugs only when things are too quiet or too noisy, or when I am asked to choose between spinach lasagna and Beef Stroganoff, or when I fill the stale air with inane revelations. "Did you know that Devil Dog spelled backwards is God lived? Did you know it takes around thirty-two years to count to one billion if you count one number per second, twenty-four hours a day? Did you know about Hitler's anatomical issues? Did you know that I can stick my tongue up my nose?"

"No," my cousin Laurie winced. "I did not know that."

And despite the insipidness of the claim, I knew that her ignorance of my talent was symbolic of something – symbolic of the fact that although we were relatives, we were also relative strangers. She didn't know a lot about me. I didn't know a lot about her.

Laurie was already six when I was a little older than zero. She was going to Beatles concerts when I was learning about fractions, graduating from college when I was running for Student Council, and getting married when I was anticipating an anthropology thesis on gender differences in Mesopotamia. And she was riding horses and tending bar while I was jamming the wonders of the quadratic formula down students' throats.

Time did what time does, however, until Laurie didn't seem that much older to me anymore, and I didn't seem that much younger to her. And time had given birth to a poignant switch – of me trying to tag along after my sister and cousin as they bicycled up our gravel driveway in exchange for the new image of my cousin tugging on my sleeve, asking me to bring her to Italy, and entreating me to introduce her to the wonders of our roots.

And that helped explain why we found each other seated next to each other in a tin can hurling through the skies – pondering the absurdities of life and the wonders of the nostril.

As we hovered over the Atlantic on our very distant approach to Rome, the blackness of the skies brought some solace to my mind. Behind us, it was night. In front, it was day. The peace outside filled the cabin with optimism and grace as we headed toward a place where both live freely.

Laurie had settled down quickly after our airline dinner of *pasta, pane, insalata mista, acqua minerale, torta, e vino rosso*. We had barely kept up with our forks' paces as the meal squelched all vestiges of hunger that had flown inside of us. We basked in the moments following our last bite and welcomed the dimming of the lights as we entered the longest phase of our trans-Atlantic route.

It was in that suspended state of satiation and altitude, between sobriety and inebriation, that Laurie and I began to traverse the boundaries of acquaintance, family, and friendship. I took a sip of the remaining red wine and licked my lips before I spoke. And I was grateful that darkness hid the risk of my questions and the invitation of emotion.

"Lau'?"

"Yes."

"Are you awake?"

"Uh-huh."

"Feel like talking?"

"Sure. I can't sleep yet."

It was then that I asked my cousin the true reason why she was seated next to me. The adventure, for certain, had been entertained for years. But over time her desire had grown stronger, until she pressed me for exact dates to make her fantasy real.

Laurie took a sip, too, before speaking, and shifted her position in the narrow seats, to settle into a comfort that would hold her words.

"I have to say that it is mostly about *nonna*," she said, slowly at first. "Our grandmother was the first one to get me interested in going to Italy. We spent a lot of time together when I was little. And Italy, whether the language or the food, was always a part of our visits." Then she paused before she continued, and her eyes fell to a spot of some consequence. "But it's also about Mom, you know," she said, more slowly still. "It's also definitely about Mom. I didn't want to keep going through life saying I wanted to do things, but never doing them...."

The silence that followed was understandable, and long, and loud.

And the darkness suddenly felt more like death than like peace.

I *knew* her answer was going to include those words, and I knew we both would welcome the chance it offered to bring her mother, my aunt, along for the ride.

For company.

For commonality.

For protection.

In the lazy silence, I knew we heard the sounds inside each other's head. That life is short. And fragile. And that there is no promise of a future.

I had learned that lesson as a niece, as the one who shared Aunt Martha's name. As the one who relished our Sunday childhood visits, her pointed humor, and her willingness to straddle the lines between dignity and irreverence. But Laurie had learned it from a closer place – as a loving daughter. A daughter who knew her mother's spirit, humor, and stoicism. A daughter who understood, in the waning weeks, days, hours, and minutes of her mother's life, that the cancer, the cancer that ravaged her lungs, would not care about any of that. And that things would change. And that things would change forever.

Laurie's thumb gently circled a spot that the wine had made on her white napkin. And then she moved her eyes to look at me. We nodded to each other and smiled, barely, before our heads turned in different directions and our bodies exhaled the pain of irreversible things.

Minutes later, I thought she had drifted off to sleep under the hum of the engines. But then she spoke again.

"Campo di Giove (Cahmpoe dee Joevay). Do you *believe* we'll be in Nonna's hometown in just a few hours?"

"I know. It's hard to believe, isn't it?"

"You know, Nonna and I used to have a great time together," she said gradually, as if working her way back through the years, clearing away the weight of all kinds of moments and picking up energy as she spoke. "She let me water her violets – the ones she kept on the white, wrought-iron cart in the living room. And she let me crank the handle on the old washing machine. And then we'd hang out the clothes to dry on the lines in the backyard. And she taught me how to say the Rosary. And how to count to ten and say the alphabet – both in Italian. I had to beg her to do those things. She'd say, 'We're in America now. We should be speaking English,' which she did flawlessly, with little hint of a foreign accent.

"But the biggest thing," Laurie continued, "is that we used to go to St. Mary's Church together and do the Stations of the Cross. She'd take my fingers into her smooth, soft hand. I can still feel how little they felt inside. Then we'd swing our arms, so slightly, as we walked up the stairs to the church. Straightening our *mantillas* just before we stepped inside.

"The church was always dark," Laurie said. "And cavernous. The only light was through the stain-glassed windows or the tiny, red candles that people lighted when they prayed. Nonna and I would walk up the center aisle and kneel when we got to the front. I would follow her. Do what she did. Watch every move she made from the corner of my eye.

"Then we'd start the Stations. Nonna's lips would move. And she would bring her rosary beads to her lips and kiss them. And bow her head. And move her lips some more. So I would move mine, too."

"Weren't you scared?"

"No," Laurie answered quickly. "I was never scared. Not when I was with Nonna. Never when I was with Nonna." She paused then, until a passenger took time to pass our seats. And then she said, "You know, I *still* miss her."

"Me, too. More than thirty years later, I still miss her, too."

And we were quiet again. So that I could let my mind admit that while I missed my grandmother – the mother of my mother and the keeper of all that a grandmother should be – I also knew that I missed what was here when she was here. Her son. Grandparents' laps. Old dogs. Patience. Hand-knit sweaters. And innocence – thirty fewer years of aging on the faces and hands, mindsets and memories, of parents and brothers and sisters, aunts, uncles, and cousins.

"Do you remember Nonna's ears?" is what Laurie said when she spoke again.

"Yes," I said smiling. "I do."

"They were so soft. Like her hands. Remember the story about her on the boat over to Ellis Island? That she wanted to be wearing earrings when she landed in the United States?"

"But she didn't have any," I said. "So she took two safety pins and put them in her ears – so that she could feel dressed up when she first stepped on the soil."

"Do you have earrings for Campo di Giove?"

"Yes. Do you?"

"Yes."

And I reached up to let my fingers graze my silver earrings. I was smiling to myself when Laurie spoke once more.

"Life is short, eh, *cugina*?" she said.

"Yes. Life is very short."

And then she reached across the arm rest and patted my hand with her own. Her hand felt soft. And my fingers felt small inside.

And before long, quietly, quietly, in the silence of memory, I drifted off to sleep, dreaming of Italian birds singing their songs under the light of the Roman moon and the spell of the bells of the local cathedral.

It never takes more than a minute in Italy to find a specimen who defines beauty. Sometimes it is a beauty of the inside – when a native wraps his arms around the present to appreciate an elder's spirit or a baby's simplicity. Other times it is a beauty of the outside – when a sculpted jaw line, bottomless eyes, or a narrow frame makes the foreigner stare before she considers her old and hideous definition of how striking the human form can be.

"I have seen more beautiful people in my first forty-six minutes in Rome than I have seen in the first forty-six years of my life," Laurie said as we fought the crowds at Leonardo da Vinci Airport. "Look," she said as our taxi driver jumped out of his car to help with our luggage. "Look at him!"

Our driver had the kind of rich, deep-dark, wavy hair that places Mediterranean inhabitants as the follicle leaders of the universe. It was so dark it looked blue, and so thick, so crested, that it made those whose lives exist outside the influence of their sun and olive oil look anemic and unfinished – like an uncooked pancake.

His jeans hung firmly on his legs of marble, and the end of his leather belt, which was too long for his tapered waist, was tucked into his jeans pocket. The sleeves of his bright-yellow, long-sleeved shirt were rolled up with precision just over his lower arms.

Within an instant, we were headed toward the heart of Rome behind a driver who exuded a relentless energy – the kind that visits those who are too far away from death to let it cross their minds and just close enough to birth to live young and fearless.

"Where are you from?" he asked us from the rear view mirror.

"*Veniamo dagli Stati Uniti*," I said. "Boston."

"Like the music group," he said, switching to Italian.

"Yes. Like the music group."

"They sang *More Than A Feeling*, didn't they? Do you know that song? *More Than A Feeling*?"

"Yes, I do. But I'm surprised *you* know it. It's old."

"*Bo*. But it's a classic, eh?"

"*Si,* it's a classic."

"Eh, *mi chiamo* Ippolito."

"It's a pleasure to meet you, Ippolito. *Mi chiamo* Marta. And this is my cousin Laura."

"For how long are you in Rome?"

"Just for a few hours, actually. We want to see Rome in the early morning light, but we will leave later today."

"Why? Why so short a stay?"

"We're heading to Campo di Giove in Abruzzo. It's the tiny village where our *nonna* was born. Both of our grandparents were born in Italy, more than 100 years before, and Laurie's father and my mother came from their marriage, after our grandparents met in the United States. We're in search of birth homes and any relatives we might find."

We were on a mission of history and roots and family.

"So, you are Italian?"

"*Si.*"

"And your *cognome*?"

"Cummings (Coomings)."

"*Coomings*? That's not Italian! Italian grandparents with a name like *Coomings*? No. No."

"My father is Irish, so I am part Irish and part Italian. But Laura and I are both Italian. Our grandparents *were* born here."

"Your mother's *cognome*?"

"My mother's name was Ragonese."

"Ahh. Rah♪Go♫Nay♪Zay♪. Rah♪Go♫Nay♪Zay♪. OK. *Brava*."

And then, with one finger on the steering wheel, he turned it sharply to the right and then to the left and then to the right again, with barely a hair's width between the headlights, windows, and doors of other cars. And then he pressed down on the accelerator and worked up enough speed to warrant his moving his hand to his forehead to whisk back the strands of hair that were dancing on his face. Then he winked in the rearview mirror and sang out…

"Rah♪Go♫Nay♪Zay♪.

"Ah, Rah♪Go♫Nay♪Zay♪."

…………

The streets surrounding the Roman train station were as I had remembered them – diverse and bouncing with activity. Tee-shirts and books and *aranciata* drinks were being sold from makeshift stands. Buses were waiting to shuttle crowds to Italian and foreign destinations. Trees were flapping their leaves in the currents. Ancient buildings rose up from the cobblestone streets and were glad to have an occasional splash from the ornate fountains that dot the city. And hundreds of automobiles were dashing about, as ready and willing participants in a human video game.

Our driver was impatient about making his own contribution to the turmoil. He worked his way into the heart of the log jam like a single-minded salmon, pressing forward, forward, until we were one of dozens of cars inching to drop off passengers at Termini.

"What is going on?" Laurie asked.

"Welcome to Rome," I answered.

"This is normal?"

"This is normal."

Within seconds of saying our good-byes to Ippolito and storing our luggage inside the station lockers, a flood of light, and sounds, and wild herbs traveled swiftly to our senses – tempting us to lean farther into the offerings of the capital city. So we did, and each of our steps along the Roman side streets punctuated our presence in a very different place and time: gilt-edged maps, ceramic fruit bowls, high-heeled sneakers, antique desks, swirling ivy, and peaches that rivaled cantaloupes in stature. We purchased two of the fruits, wrapped in thin brown paper, had the first of the country's *cappuccino*, and meandered through the early hours with heavenly flavors bouncing on top of our taste buds, stepping aimlessly toward a morning of freedom.

As the juices of the peaches skimmed our lips, we sauntered, but sometimes skipped, to follow whatever paths our eyes chose. Our walk took us alongside San Pietro in Vicoli, where Michelangelo's Moses has horns and academicians hover to search for a spiritual or human explanation. We were dwarfed by the walls that lead to the Circus Maximus and comforted by the shade of the cypress trees that line up in order throughout the city. Our hands visited fountains and were cooled by the waters that pour from a sculpture's mouth or hands or wings. We smelled the needles of aging trees, touched the façades of ancient domiciles, rested briefly on stone benches to turn our faces to the sun, and smacked our lips to revisit the shades of peach and *cappuccino*.

Our first hours in Italy unfolded without order, without a plan, until we realized that something had certainly been in charge of our aimlessness – for the highest reaches of the Coliseum had watched our every move and had gestured us along, pulling us in, knowing that, in time, all paths lead to its doors.

The Coliseum's uppermost tier, dressed in Corinthian elegance given its proximity to the heavens, was the first thing to peak above the cypress trees. Its visit was refined and fell humbly on our unsuspecting eyes. With my back and neck arched, I remembered my *first* view of the Coliseum from the near seat of an airport bus. I had wept as we skirted by, twisting my head from inside my cloud of disbelief. How, how, how could it be that I am under the umbrella of the Coliseum, I had whispered.

Laurie, instead, would have her first glimpse from its shadows. She would stand in its power and let her arms extend so that her hands could touch the stone and feel the history of architecture, sacrifice, and a culture that had given birth to our grandmother Beatrice and our grandfather Antonio.

We moved slowly once it had come into view, taking note of the meticulous stone walls and the trees with the rich green, mushroomed tops that flank the path to its side. Tiny cars raced by with drivers' eyes fixated on roads and speedometers instead of on the beauty that encircled them. Beauty of all kinds was quite ordinary for the Romans, where the Coliseum's primary function was to be a landmark more than a thing to which they should herd themselves.

I heard Laurie skip a breath and stop mid-step when the shape took clearer form in front of us – moving from occupying a fraction of our view to nearly all of it. It was not long before I saw her tears, through my tears, flowing down her cheeks and left untouched as she stared upward.

As the opening hours of our trip unfolded and as my cousin began to send messages about what moved her, her tears suggested that she might be more drawn to things that *aren't* back home than things that are. It was a layer I was happy to peel back as she grew more familiar.

Laurie and I became quiet, and we separated. In the silence, I looked up above the Coliseum to the azure skies and imagined my *nonna*, soft, sometimes serious, with waves of gray hair, and my *nonno*, with angled face, earnest eyes, and a mask over the humor that rested within. I knew they were smiling on us, the youngest granddaughters in each family, and extending their arms around our shoulders. We are proud of you, I felt them say, and glad you are here, with us.

Laurie was still crying when we met again, and she said she wanted to call her home and share the moment with those who'd never been. I understood, but no, I thought, first to myself, and then aloud into my cousin's ears. "Be here. Be here, *cugina*, for this moment will too quickly pass. And you will long for it when you are far away."

"You're right," she said, and looked up to the sky, and let the sun shine warm against her skin. And there we remained, without watches, without schedules, lounging in the power of the Coliseum.

It was Laurie's first time.

It was, I think, my twentieth.

She was thrilled because she hadn't known what to expect.

I was thrilled because I did.

Chapter Two

D A N C E S

Campo di Giove, Abruzzo

The car rental agency in the heart of Termini Station had us registered and in a Fiat within minutes of our return from the Coliseum. Air-conditioning, power locks, an alarm system, a tape deck, and extremely prompt service hinted at an efficiency that was ordinarily foreign to Rome.

Since I had visited the city numerous times before, we determined that I should climb in behind the wheel in that I would have some advantage of familiarity. "It's easy. It's easy," the employee at the rental agency had said, handing us a map and drawing a very direct line out of the station's parking lot to the street that would lead us away from Rome and toward Abruzzo.

I ignited the engine, slipped in an Eros Ramazzotti cassette, and pulled out of Termini with confidence. And as I watched the trees that surround the station flutter their good-byes, I relished the notion that, for some, Rome is the center of the world, but for us, it was merely a steppingstone on the path to our roots.

Thirty seconds later, the relish vanished when we missed our first turn and stormed full-speed ahead into a parking lot that was mined with cypress-trees-in-a-box. Sweat began to trickle along my temples when a startled, orange-clad sanitation worker dropped his wooden rake to signal our wrong-way route on a one-way street and used both of his fists to offer a cultural gesture and a more direct route out of the city.

Eros Ramazzotti was silenced and tossed to the Fiat carpet, and our hearts pounded as we inched toward a Roman roundabout that, minutes later, had us locked inside and left us speculating that we would spend the entire two weeks of our vacation traveling in circles, sandwiched in-between Italian trucks exuding poisonous exhaust.

In time, an irrational departure from the roundabout led us to a tiny sign pointing us toward Route A-24 that would lead to A-25, the major highway to Abruzzo. Only one hour after we had left Termini, which was approximately fifty-one minutes longer than it would have taken a native, the anarchy of the capital city's streets had been replaced by a meticulous and stunning freeway, where mountains and blue skies were the norm and where cypress-trees-in-a-box were nowhere to be found. What was to be found, however, was the first sign for the region of our grandmother.

Abruzzo.

And the hometown of our grandmother.

Campo di Giove.

PRATOLA P
uscita
SULMONA

► CORFINIO – RAIANO
► CAMPO DI GIOVE
► Parco Nazionale della Maiella
► ROCCARASO
► CASTEL DI SANGRO

500 m

Campo di Giove.

They were words I had heard since my earliest inquiries.

Where was Nonna born?

In Campo di Giove. In Abruzzo.

But when I heard those words, or spoke them as a child, only the letters presented themselves in my imagination. Black letters rising up and down against the white screen of my mind.

CAHM-POE DEE JOE-VAY
AH-BREWTS-O

No images. No sense that Campo di Giove was a real place with real people that still thrived after my grandmother had left. How could it have? She was gone from there, and life only existed within the boundaries of my vision. It was only my *nonna* who was real.

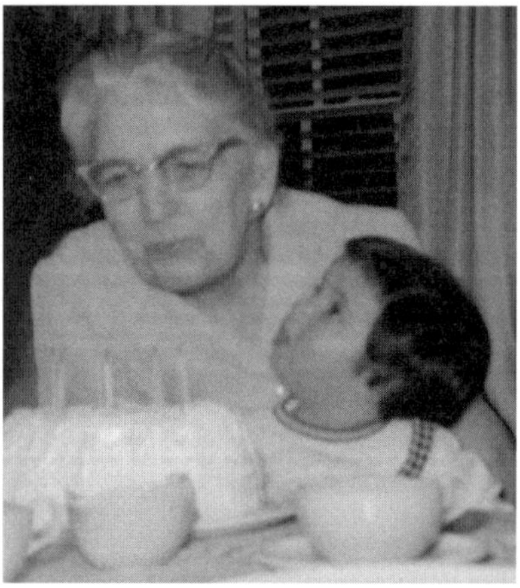

I used to tickle her big toes through her open-ended shoes and sit on her lap to welcome her arms and hands around me. I would beg for her homemade broth with the tiny *pastina.* Weave my fingers through her soft, gray hair. And look at her with admiration, as if aware, somehow, of the speed with which those minutes would disappear.

When I saw my grandmother, I saw her only as a grandmother, an American grandmother, and not as a grandmother who had come from Campo di Giove.

Campo di Giove.

They were just letters dancing in my head.

Until they disappeared in 1968, on the day my *nonna* died. I was only nine when the mother of my mother went away. And when I watched *my* mother pound the countertop, I knew I was seeing what kind of mother my grandmother had been, and what kind of mother *her* mother had been. Back, back, back into the roots of Campo di Giove. In Abruzzo.

And then finally, just after the letters disappeared for what I thought was forever, I wondered where Campo di Giove was and where Abruzzo was. But thirty years later, they were facing me again, dancing again, inside my head and in my line of vision. On a sky-blue sign on an Italian highway, surrounded by fresh air and a history we were bound to uncover.

The excitement of glimpsing the letters pulled us off the highway to smaller roads and hairpin turns, well-manicured farm land, and dormant ski resorts, stripped by the autumn heat. The guidebooks had spoken of an extreme poverty and desolation, and the nearly-abandoned town that first greeted us seemed to confirm those decrees. But I, instead, was overcome by a richness of humanity – a richness that immediately welcomed us, as residents leaned out their windows or approached our car to answer our question about the existence of restaurants in their tiny village.

"*No, non ci sono ristoranti qui,*" the gentleman said as he smiled and leaned into the driver side of the Fiat – in a way that was more welcoming than obtrusive. And then he offered explicit directions to a restaurant down the road.

So we nodded and drove away, and we waved as the Italians do, by pulling our four fingers toward us. I caught Laurie comparing *our* national gesture to *theirs* by practicing the flow of fingers on our new friends. When she turned to me and smiled, I knew she was enamored and had noted that the subtleties of life are not so subtle after all.

The *ristorante* the man had described sprang up out of nowhere – on the far fringes of a quiet village that was winding down for the lunch hour. When we parked the car and walked toward the smells of garlic and breads, the fresh air of the mountains pierced our lungs and let us know that Rome was far away.

Everything inside suggested a local clientele – where English was not heard, clothing was rustic, and a hearty décor was in line with its remote locale. Cheeses and meats hung from the rafters. Heavy wooden tables complemented the alpine exterior. And large, dented, metal pots played host to offerings that were more equipped to battle the region's chills.

We ordered two of Nonna's specialties and embraced the habit of requesting a liter of the house wine and *acqua minerale.* When the glasses were filled, we clinked them and offered a toast to our vacation, to our dreams, and to Nonna and Nonno. And to Laurie's parents – my Aunt Martha and Uncle Angelo Vincent (Uncle Vin) – who, we knew, would rally their collective forces to watch over us.

Laurie's *gnocchi* arrived and my *pasta e fagioli* followed immediately. The presentation of each was accompanied by a proper and operatic pronunciation by our Abruzzese waiter – whose native tongue succeeded in snuffing out the butchered manner in which the tiny pillow-pasta and soup are pronounced back home. Ganokey and Pasta Fajoo were not welcomed there.

Unabashed culinary moans and prolonged periods of closed eyelids filled our space as each spoonful of my soup and the tomato-and-basil-dressed *gnocchi* met Laurie's mouth. In a family of mothers and fathers and aunts and uncles and daughters and sons and cousins who live in a perpetual state of being either "stahvin'" or "stuffed," a miracle of patience and appreciation was unfolding in the hills of Abruzzo – as food was emerging as a gift to be savored and whose flavors should be discerned, and not as a thing to be swallowed whole to fill a hole.

When we rose from the table two hours later, after a medley of local cheeses, *dolci*, and *caffè*, we pushed through the mahogany doors and into the brisk, clean air – feeling nurtured, again, by our grandmother. It was the first time, in a very long time, that we had tasted her cooking, and we were relieved to discover that we, and they, had not forgotten.

....

Sunshine and rich, cloudless, sapphire skies beckoned us up, up to Campo di Giove after our lunch, as did windy, s-shaped lanes that led us high into the mountains. With each second that slipped by, it grew clearer that we were moving toward our grandmother's obscure birthplace. The trend-setting fashions of the capital city had been replaced with the customs of the Old World. Women wrapped themselves in the blackness of mourners so that strangers would know how to treat them until time had time to heal. Wrinkled-faced men, with hand-carved canes, strode next to their donkeys as their parcels of wheat were carried upward. Elderly grandmothers sculpted their hair into tiny buns, wore cat-eye glasses with black trim, and maneuvered the streets in shoes where big toes poked out and heels hindered their progress. Four different familial generations held hands in the streets and loved to while away the hours in sartorial splendor. And groups of men of all ages collected themselves at round bar tables, sipped *espresso*, stared relentlessly, and scrutinized the wavelets of activity in the tiny hamlets that surround Campo di Giove.

Time moved strangely as we grew closer.

Each second felt as long as a minute. Each minute as long as an hour. Nonna's region slowed us and taunted us with its dizzying drops, crowds of pine trees, and steep rises alongside near-circular bends – but then soothed us with its endless vistas and by building our expectations of the land that rests just below the heavens.

Laurie and I were quiet inside the car. I trust we were weighing the disbelief of its imminence. The surreal nature of having something long-denied rise up in front of us for the taking. For the breathing. For the swallowing.

Laurie's head turned toward the right then. I saw her shaking it from side-to-side as she looked at the magnificence that enveloped us from each one of the 360 degrees. But this, I knew we knew, was a different beauty. It was a beauty that had been touched by our grandmother, and abandoned by our grandmother, as the women in her family held hands and walked toward something they believed to be better.

But what, I thought, could be better than this.

Then one last turn brought us into full view of our wants.

Benvenuti a Campo di Giove

Welcome to Campo di Giove.

We wended our way through the periphery of town to a parking space just down from the main *piazza*, a most serene Italian feature, where cars are banned, walks are encouraged, townsfolk are sought out, and the ripples of life are examined outside the earshot of noisy motorcycles.

Our arrival, however, did not cause a ripple.

Our arrival caused a *tsunami*.

My ankle had barely slipped through the crevice between car and street when all eyes were upon us. The round table of men had grown from two to four. The bar owner was poking his head through hanging beads. And three perpetual mourners, widows of the ages, were feigning a conversation over the red geraniums that decorated their window boxes.

Laurie nodded to me in their direction.

"*Buon giorno, Signore*," I called out.

"*Buon giorno, Signorine*," they replied.

"*Come state oggi?*"

"*Bene. Bene, grazie. E tu?*" they called back to me, with what I thought to be a hint of surprise that Italian was being exchanged. I answered that I was doing well, thank you, and that it was a beautiful day and that the air felt so clean and that we had just driven in from Rome. And then I reached into the car to get my backpack before I locked the doors, glanced back up at the three who had not budged from their positions of inspection, and decided to continue our exchange – always in Italian.

"Can you guess why we're here, *Signore*? Why it is that we came all the way from our homes to Campo di Giove?"

My question was abruptly replaced with a classic and silent Italian retort – where lips are pursed, eyebrows are moved inward, the brow is creased, and the front of the face is pushed forward in a singular jerking motion, while the hands are cupped, stretching fingers to thumbs, before being thrust upward in the direction of the clouds.

The Italian gesture screams a clear meaning.

No, of course we do not know why you're here. So, hurry up, and tell us because we want to know everything that is going on, and we don't want to waste too much time waiting to find out because there is little else going on here, and this is the most excitement we have had in weeks. Furthermore, we want to be the first ones to find out so that when it spreads around the whole town that you are here we can tell people that we were the first to know and that we knew long before everyone else and that *we* even knew why you were here before *you* even knew why you were here. So enough with the games and tell these three old, old, and getting older-by-the-minute women why you are here, *Signorina*. Hmmph.

So, I did.

"My grandmother, the mother of my mother, was born here, right here, in Campo di Giove, more than 100 years ago."

This was big.

Very big.

"*Il suo nome*?"

"She was a Rubeo, and her mother was a Fiorinanni."

"Ooooh, Rubeo, Rubeo, Fiorinanni, Fiorinanni," they shrieked, in bold spite of their somber clothes. And then they conferred for quite a spell, while their heads shook and nodded, and their fingers pointed and stirred up the atmosphere, and their hands clapped as they yelled out discord and accord and discord again before finally rendering a verdict.

"Rubeo – *no*. Fiorinanni – *no*."

"*No*?"

"Those names used to be here. But no longer. The last Rubeo was here many, many years ago. They moved away to other parts. The last Fiorinanni was here until recently. Domenico Fiorinanni. But he died two years ago. He used to live right there, in that house on the corner. But he was the last one."

Laurie and I barely had time to react to the shattering news when we realized that standing behind us now, having sneaked up during our brief exchange with the triumvirate, were three more people: a poster child for the elderly Italian woman (hair bun, cat-eye glasses, black dress, and open-toed clunkers), her striking grandson, whose elbow served as a willing shelf to his *nonna's* wrinkled hand, and from the table in front of the bar, a man, with rich, gray hair and a conservative presentation of black pants with a classic striped shirt.

"*Why* are you here?" the last asked, trapping a tone between entitlement, gentility, and strict curiosity. "Oh," he said after we had filled him in. "That's interesting. That's very interesting." And then, oh so slowly and oh so casually, in perfect British, "My name is Angelo. Rest here. I will return *subito* with my wife's aunt. She'll know everything you need to know about the Fiorinanni and Rubeo lines." And he darted up the main street leading away from the *piazza*.

The resultant conversation of the geranium-sentries had the energy of boiling atoms as they amended their research to include not only those whose last names were Rubeo or Fiorinanni but also those whose lineage included either one. But we had already lost faith in their thoroughness and waited for Angelo to return with some news.

We looked up to find him strolling down the lane, arm-in-arm, with a woman nearing seventy years – Iolanda (Yolanda), his wife's aunt. She was outfitted to the nines in a blue and gold silky dress that buttoned up the front and fell just below her knees, a long blue sweater with gold buttons, stockings, and matching leather shoes. Her heels did little to help her break the five-foot mark, and her brown hair, parted naturally in the middle, fell flat on her head.

When the four of us met at the edge of the *piazza*, Angelo introduced us and then asked his aunt the name of her grandmother. The first word that Iolanda spoke was simple.

And powerful.

And perfect.

"Rubeo. The name of my grandmother was Lucia Rubeo."

The name brushed off our ears and into the winds of Campo di Giove. Roo♪Bay♫Oh♪. Perhaps within range of where our *nonna* had been raised and schooled, had played and placed her tiny toes. "The name of my grandmother was Lucia Rubeo," she had said. "Roo♪Bay♫Oh♪."

"What?" I asked, first facing Iolanda, and then facing Laurie, and then Iolanda again. "What did she say? Did she say Rubeo? Did you say Rubeo? Did you say your grandmother's name was Lucia Rubeo?"

"Yes. Rubeo."

"Could it be the same Rubeo as our *nonna*? Beatrice Rubeo?"

"Tsst. Of course, of course. This is a small village."

"And do you know the name Fiorinanni?"

"Yes. Rubeo. Fiorinanni. Yes, they are both old Campo di Giove families. Come. Come up to my house. Let's have some tea, and we will find the answers to your questions."

"Lau'," I murmured, as Angelo parted company with Iolanda and returned to his real estate on the main *piazza*, "how about *his* name?"

"Angelo?"

"Yah."

"Same as my dad's."

"Do you know what it means in Italian? It means angel."

"Angel. I like that," Laurie said smiling. "I like that a lot."

....

Iolanda's tour of the marble-floored living room, three bedrooms, kitchenette, and bathroom was filled with pride. She opened each door of her armoire, pulled back the blinds overlooking her balcony to expose the sun-soaked rolling hills, fluffed the pillows on her living room sofa, picked a speck of dust from the mahogany table, and waited for our reaction to her family home of 435 years.

We were suitably respectful of what she owned and how she maintained it, what she remembered and how she preserved it, what she said and how she presented it. Especially when she spoke of her father.

Tears welled up in her eyes when she remembered him, long since deceased – the father who spent some time in America before he returned to Campo di Giove for the comfort he had missed. The Italian-English dictionary he had used when he crossed to "the other side" was her most prized possession and was held like a newborn child. She passed the tattered volume to me, and I could feel his hopes in those pages and in the words that struggled to bridge the gaps of culture and serenity.

Over tea, Iolanda unfolded the history of her life and, in some distant way, our lives. It was not long before we learned our connection – that her grandmother, Lucia Rubeo, and our great-grandfather, Vincenzo Rubeo, were sister and brother, and that her father, who experimented with the new world, and our *nonna*, who bid good-bye to the old one, were first cousins, and that my mother, Antoinette Frances, and my mother's brother, Angelo Vincent, and Iolanda, were second cousins.

I interrupted her discourse only to search for my journal, the journal that was littered with the memories and discoveries of two decades – from my early twenties through my thirties and into my forties. It contained the spent train ticket from my first trip to Italy, a *New Yorker* cartoon that read, "Martha hates clutter," a business card from the best place to buy gloves in Florence, and a sketch of the Greek ruins in Segesta. It harbored random thoughts about the deaths of friends' parents, the wonders of teaching, my frustrations with poor visionaries, and the diagnosis of a brain tumor in a friend – a friend who still makes me laugh as hard and as openly as I did when I was a child. It was filled with the privilege of privacy and the embarrassment of the same. And then, right then, it was being filled with the path to my past – with the branches of a genealogical tree.

Iolanda spied as I sketched the details onto the blocked pages. Occasionally, she checked her watch, pulled up her sleeves, examined my Italian spelling, offered us a cold drink, and checked her watch again, while punctuating the facts with old memories. On her final check of the time, I asked if we were keeping her from something – if we had interrupted a routine.

"Well," she said, "I usually go to church each day at this time. Do you, would you like to, do you want to go to church with me?" she asked, with a tilt of her head and a glimpse of fear that the two heathens from America might actually say no.

Despite the chasm between Laurie's familiarity with my world and my familiarity with hers, I was fairly certain that church was not a part of either of our routines. That church was something we did on holidays, if so compelled, and something we had done when we had been under the thumbs of our parents. But that church was something that had disappeared once we had eluded our parents' traditions. Notwithstanding all of that, we heard ourselves saying, "Yes. Yes. We would like to go to church."

Iolanda left the room and returned seconds later in a different outfit, as if her previous one had needed any renovation. We, on the other hand, were at the opposite end of the fashion spectrum – in jeans, windbreakers, and hiking boots. But Iolanda ushered us out of her double doors using her hands as shovels and her voice as a prod.

Punctuality, apparently, was more important than appearance.

We weren't long outside when we realized we were in a parade – a parade of possession. Iolanda owned the greatest news of the day, the month, maybe the year. We marched the slope from her home to *La Chiesa di Sant'Eustachio* and watched the heads poke out their windows as we moved forward. One-by-one they appeared and then retreated in a kind of Cranial Domino.

La Chiesa di Sant'Eustachio rested at the bottom of the tiny hill, just beyond the *piazza* where Laurie and I had first settled in Campo di Giove. Its spire held a large clock with Roman numerals, an old bell, and a pyramidal top, whose light complexion was stark in its contrast to the blue skies. Trees, ivy, and tiny plantings further softened the quaint church's entrance.

Inside, the church was dark, except for the altar, which radiated light from the small, rectangular window just behind. Wooden pews, fifteen on each side, cushioned the faithful, and murals and oil paintings told the story of Christ's journey to death. The living were scattered around the church singularly or in groups of two to three. All women, half of them dressed in black, most with white hair.

Laurie and I hunkered next to each other, and Iolanda perched near Laurie. In sitting side-by-side, Laurie and I were doing something from which her brother, Tom, and I had been forever banned since childhood. Our mothers issued that pronouncement after a bout of hysteria in a New Hampshire chapel, when Tom and I rose when we heard a certain "It's Time To Stand Now" inflection in the lector's voice. Seconds later, we scanned the congregation to find that we were the *only* two standing. When we fell to our seats, embarrassment and fits of laughter consumed us. Tom's mother, my Aunt Martha, stood, quietly, and slipped in-between Tom and me, saying nothing. But the gesture, from a woman who rarely, if ever, lost her patience, was deafening.

Ironically, years later, it was Aunt Martha who needed the sharp reprimand. It happened when I leaned over to ask her if the priest were about to start the Homily – which I mistakenly pronounced Hoe-mily. She leaned back and said, "Martha, dear, this is the Hawmily. *You* are Hoe-mily." In the midst of the eruption that followed, my mother stood, quietly, and slipped herself in-between my aunt and me, saying nothing. But the gesture, again, from another woman who rarely, if ever, lost her patience, could not have been more deafening.

As a result, I knew to avoid the entire Ragonese family when in church, and I had succeeded for many years. But as the Campo di Giove priest made his way to the podium, I was newly haunted by the perils of sitting next to *another* Ragonese in a place of worship.

Until the *parroco's* visage came into full view.

His hunched appearance underscored his lengthy years and his poor state of health. His cough confirmed the latter even more. Two altar boys, dressed in the costume of the old, flanked him – both as part of the ritual and as security to his frailty. His tone was abrupt, peeved, and expected by the local clientele.

He moved through the readings and the Homily in record speed. And before we knew it, after a handful of agitated announcements about upcoming parish events, the priest concluded the Mass, blessed us from above, and shuffled away to his vestibule to the left.

Iolanda nodded that the Mass was officially over and then asked us if we would like her to appeal to the priest to look at the old church documents, stored just off the altar. She was certain that the volumes held details of baptisms and marriages and might provide some answers to our genealogical search.

After allowing the priest a minute or two to change out of his robes, she rambled up to the vestibule while we waited in our pews, ever mindful of the gentle stares of those around us. When Iolanda resurfaced, she waved her arm and hand, and we walked slowly to the front.

The priest was no more soothing up close than he had been from far away. My knees did an involuntary genuflection when we were introduced, and my stomach did some of the same when he failed to hide his annoyance at the request that would prolong his duties for the day.

That, I knew, was the Italian way.

But in the end, I knew he would come through.

That, too, is the Italian way.

"What are you looking for?" he asked.

"Anything having to do with our grandmother. I know her name and the date of her birth. Beatrice Rubeo – 16 March 1887. And I know the names and wedding date of her parents. Vincenzo Rubeo and Lucia Fiorinanni – 24 July 1883."

He shook his head back and forth and moved toward a tiny room off the vestibule. From there, he croaked out that we would have trouble reading the documentation, even if he could find it. "It's in old Italian. And Latin," he barked. Iolanda's face reddened slightly, and we shrugged.

That, of course, did not matter to us. What mattered was that we might be standing in the church where our great-grandparents had been married and where our *nonna* was baptized, and that we might, in the next several minutes, be looking straight at the ancient documents that confirm that reality.

We waited.

He grunted every now and then.

And then he emerged from the side with a Book of Marriages in his hand. He placed it on the table, a wooden piece that had been painted in swirling greens and reds and yellows, and flopped open the pages of the book with a hint of impatience.

One-by-one I turned the off-white sheets, etched with a black fountain pen in twisting patterns. Their age made a sound, the crinkling, fragile sound of parchment, as we moved closer to the year that had some meaning to us – 1879, 1880, 1881, 1882, 1883. And then closer to the month, and then closer to the day.

Hope and cynicism lived side-by-side in that tiny chapel and battled each other with each turn of the page and each spill of the pen that left us without a view of their names.

Laurie and I bent our bodies over the book – scanning the words furtively for something familiar, something that was a part of us, that would tie us to this place, this town, and this country. Something that we could share with my mother and my mother's sister, Aunt Lucille, when we returned home.

Something new.

Something old.

When that something surfaced, our eyes landed on the words at the same time – nestled between two other families' precious beginnings and next to the details of the wedding day in the language of the learned.

Vincentium Rubeo
et
Luciaum Fiore Nanni

My eyes tried to focus on the script that spelled the Latin versions of their names, but tears began to veil my vision as I painted an imagined portrait of my *nonna's* young and stunning parents – Lucia, in a simple, but elegant, white gown, and Vincenzo, by her side, in a dark suit. I knew then that they had stood on the altar that we had just visited and that the witnesses to their matrimony had been seated in the very pews that held us during Mass.

The veil of tears quickly turned to a blanket of the same as emotion swept over my eyes and down my cheeks, spurred on by the reality of touch – the permanent reality of touch. That we were standing where they had stood, talking where they had talked, and breathing where they had breathed. That *our* dream was beginning where *their* dreams had begun.

It was the touch that weakened my knees and sent tremors through my core – tremors that were intellectually irrational but emotionally divine. For I was, in some way, touching my grandmother again and, in turn, touching the people whom she had touched. My finger held firmly to the dignity of the script and the truth of my history. My other hand steadied my position against the table and readied me for a glimpse of my cousins' faces, Laurie and Iolanda, as we each lived the beauty of the moment in ways that were unique and right for us.

When Laurie's glance met my own, I was aware that the unknown details since our childhood, the yet undiscovered nuances of each other's recent past, were dwarfed in importance by the enormity of the present. Her face had grown pale, and her slightly-opened mouth spoke no words. Glistening eyes did all the talking. We knew, already, in the stillness of our stare, that the richness of this journey would be impossible to explain and impossible to be grasped by anyone who was not with us just then, in that chamber, off that altar, of *La Chiesa di Sant'Eustachio.*

Iolanda moved forward and in-between us then, and brought her hands to rest up under our elbows. Together, our flesh forged bridges and bonds that had long been erased.

Unexpectedly, the priest approached us and leaned into the page to offer a translation. I was sure that his palpable shift in interest and kindness had been spurred by magic.

The magic of our having found a piece of buried history.

The magic of genuine passion.

He tried to read the words aloud but struggled with the legibility of the script and his own grasp of the more aged languages. He was saddened by his discovery that the barriers were even too tall for *him* to surmount. So, as if to compensate, he returned to his archive and reappeared shortly thereafter with a Book of Baptisms.

The priest searched the pages himself, with his arthritic fingers lifting the earliest sketches of people's lives and resting them one on top of the other. He stopped only to rub his eyes with his tired hands, but then he would lean forward some more, into the text, with one eye closer to the surface than the other, to try to uncover the record of our grandmother's divine approval.

Sweat gathered on his forehead. He reached up to wipe it with a satin cloth. His speech was altered by the dryness of his cough. But still, still, he leaned forward some more, into the text, with one eye closer, closer to the surface. And then he found it...

Beatrice Elia Rubeo

... and the searing, unabashed depth of our emotion convinced him that the translation did not matter. What mattered was this flame of reconnection, and the fact that two granddaughters, two great-granddaughters, had found an important piece in the reconstruction of a not-so-distant past. That we were standing in a place where our great-grandparents, Vincentium Rubeo and Luciaum Fiore Nanni, had begun the union that would lead to our existence. Where our infant *nonna* had been anointed with the traditions of her roots.

What mattered was that my images of their burial places in the United States, reminiscent of their earthly ends, were now being shared with images of their baptism and wedding in Italia, symbolic of their earthly starts.

What mattered was the moment,
and the unparalleled joys of living,
and breathing, and singing, from inside.

Before we left *La Chiesa di Sant'Eustachio*, the cousins, *le cugine*, new and old – old and young, stopped at the marble baptismal font at the front of the church. We hadn't given it a moment's notice on the way in, but on the way out, passing it by without a healthy pause was inconceivable. We swallowed up its Ionic features, the curly-haired cherub on the base, and water stains that hundreds of years of baptisms had brought to its face since its own birth of 1587.

When our fingertips moved in to caress the marble, we knew we were touching the same font of our *nonna's* infancy, where she, and most likely her parents, and their parents, and theirs, and theirs, again, had floated under the chants of a priest who welcomed their arrival to his lifetime passion. And we knew we were touching the same font of our grandmother's youth – down to its base, where she would bring the holy water to her forehead, to her heart, to her shoulder, and to her shoulder again, in prayer. So Laurie and I reached in to search for our chance to do the same. And despite its emptiness, the thirsty emptiness of years long-since replaced, the font felt cool and moist and filled.

Chapter Three

M A G I C

Campo di Giove, Abruzzo

Iolanda changed her outfit immediately after church, thereby successfully sporting half as many variations of clothing in our first day in Campo di Giove as we had brought for our whole trip. She emerged from her bedroom with the top button of her sweater nestled in slot three and the bottom button flopping aimlessly against her thigh. Despite the enormous height difference between Iolanda and Laurie, the latter's gesture was gentle when she put her arm around her older cousin to tell her about the imbalance. Iolanda laughed out loud as her small, soft cheeks reddened, and her hands flew to the spot to correct the confusion. And then she quickly offered us a place to sleep in her home – in beds that share a room with her father's sacred dictionary.

Laurie and I read each other's unspoken answer to the question – that we were grateful, but exhausted, and needed some solitude to process all the events of that day. Very little of our silent conversation was shared with Iolanda – only our appreciation of her generosity and her unencumbered trust of relative strangers.

We promised we would look her up the next day. So with a touch of sadness in her eyes, she sent us on our way and made us reconfirm, three or seven or twenty-one times, that we would see her again before we left Campo di Giove.

We promised.

....

The village quality to Campo di Giove belies its hotel offerings. In season, the town transforms itself into a haven for skiers and skaters and chalet-dwellers. The population shifts from a low-season minimum of 900 to a high-season maximum of 10,000. We settled on a three-star hotel that, like everything, was just a two-minute drive from the main *piazza*.

The hotel was surrounded by trees and dozens of squirrels searching for any remnants of food before the rush of winter. When we pulled in and parked our Fiat, the car tally in the lot was one. Laurie waited outside while I went in to inquire about room availability. A gentleman with salt and pepper hair and the latest model of designer glasses presented himself as Domenico when I rang the outdoor buzzer and then assured me that the hotel was open and that we were welcomed.

"How many rooms are there here?"

"There are 128 beds."

"How many will be filled tonight?"

"Two."

"Just us?"

"Just you."

"You will open the hotel just for us?"

"I will open the hotel just for you. But," he went on to add, "there are two problems. First, the heater is not yet turned on. It is only October and too early in the season. Second, the dining room is closed. That problem I can solve. I invite you to have dinner with my son, Sebastiano, and me. It will be simple, but we would love the pleasure of your company."

We dragged our belongings up the majestic, curved, and carpeted steps to the landing that lived just under a cathedral ceiling. Views of mountains and the interior echoes of desolation led us to the far end of the first floor, alongside ivory-colored walls with masculine wallpaper. Twin beds greeted us inside and were the perfect pre-dinner medicine for our first-day exhaustion.

"If this is all happening our first day," Laurie asked as she plopped herself down onto the mattress, "what else could possibly happen?

"Just look at what's gone on so far. We drive our way out of Rome without serious injury. We stop for lunch in Carsoli and have a meal to die for. We arrive in Campo di Giove and meet the husband of a relative in the first five minutes. He introduces us to our parents' second cousin. She takes us to Mass and brings us back to meet the priest. He shows us the ancient documentation of our great-grand-parents' wedding and our *nonna's* baptism. Iolanda asks us to stay with her. And then Domenico opens up his hotel for us and offers to feed us. We have angels. I'm telling you, Marty. I think we have angels."

And then Laurie slipped under the blanket to warm herself in the crisp early evening mountain air that had nosed its way into our room. And we waited for the announcement of dinner.

That announcement came with a sharp rap on the door and then a tiny voice. "We are ready to dine now, *Signore*. My father wonders if we may still expect you at our table. He hopes so. I hope so."

Our dining area was a shadow of what it would be in just a handful of weeks – when it would take on the airs of a ski lodge, with roaring fire and a crowd of exhausted but exhilarated skiers. Several tables were pushed to the perimeter, tablecloths were folded in the corner, and our voices would have echoed off the wooden walls if they could have been heard over the boom of the big screen television.

The Italian news was on, and in a flurry of cadence and gesticulation, men and women brought madness to our dinner with a fast-paced delivery and a no-nonsense façade. The news stories were enhanced by explanations from Domenico – who helped move us a bit further away from our tourist ranking toward a richer understanding of what makes Italy beat.

Domenico and Sebastiano had decorated the linen-covered table with what they described as a simple meal: wine, mineral water, bread, homemade pasta with homemade sauce, veal, roasted potatoes, *scamorza* cheese, and *parmigiano*. From time to time, either father or son would pick up a platter and nod his head for us to take some more. For us to fill our plates with theirs.

The television, though softened once the food started its tour of the wooden table, filled the void of minimal conversation – a void that was sparked by our stranger status and reinforced by linguistic barriers. Clearly, the relative silence could have been broken by Sebastiano speaking effortlessly with his dad, a handsome, seasoned version of his seraphic son, and by Laurie and me doing the same.

But we all knew, without stating it, that those exchanges would have set up a parallel universe, where worlds would not coincide and sameness would rest with sameness. It was a cultural reality I recognized and, to some degree, understood; but it was *not* a cultural reality I wished to perpetuate when I could do something to change it – by crossing the border between their family and our family, their language and our language, and immersing myself in their words.

So I played a kind of verbal tennis, back and forth, back and forth, between ideas and conversations – sharing only those things that seemed important or worth the translation. I focused my eyes and ears on their every syllable, every gesture, every breath, to discern the meaning of their sentiments so that I could turn to Laurie to keep her connected to the present. And when any of it, or all of it, proved too tedious, too endless, too much to bear for even one more moment, a spot of alcohol was swallowed to soften the urgency of exhaustion and confusion.

It was on the second pour from the wine bottle that Laurie noticed the label. *Aragona*. I had never seen that brand before, but I had seen the root – as in Aragon, European aristocrats, whose name, at some point, shifted to Aragona and then Aragonese and then Ragonese, the *cognome* of our past and present.

"We are royalty. Royalty," one of my Sicilian cousins would cry out with seriousness and humor during my visits to her island.

"Angels," Laurie said with the wine bottle in her hand.

"Angels?" Sebastiano said, in English.

"You speak *English*?" I asked when I turned to him.

"A bit. My mother is British."

"Does your dad speak English?"

"Not really. We spoke Italian at home."

I could not help but smile, almost smirk, as I pictured the relegation of English to second-class citizen in their household. Although fluency in English represented, to a certain extent, power and liberty throughout much of the world, Domenico's preservation of Italian delayed its extinction and set up a kind of David and Goliath dynamic – where, true to form, David had slung his shot and brought Goliath to his knees.

"*Bravo. Bravo,*" I said, first to Sebastiano and then to Domenico. The elder's smile and nod confirmed a kind of subtle victory in the battle of cultures, as well as an appreciation of *my* appreciation of the underdog.

Later in the evening, however, long after the *Aragona* had eroded the barriers of language, I learned that Domenico's marriage had ended in divorce. My short-lived happiness was forced to replace itself, again, with the angst of a tireless norm. That those who are accustomed to power often resort to a privileged disdain of those who try to dethrone them.

....

A short after-dinner drive to the local bar led to pre-fabricated *gelato*, the Italian Nutty Buddy, and an after-dinner Averna – a licorice shot that cleans the palate and helps with digestion. Its warmth was nudged aside by the evening air in Campo di Giove, which nibbled at our lungs. The scent of the pines happily climbed up and into our noses, reminding Laurie and me that we were far from our normal city and beachside dwellings.

The pine needles, though, did more than remind me of where I was. They reminded me of much earlier times, when the smell of the Christmas tree would waft through our living room and past our stockings, up the central stairs to the bedroom I shared with my sister Cindy – when my only worries on Christmas Day were whether I would get my Tony the Pony, whether Cindy would enjoy The Patti Duke Board Game I had bought for her, or whether Nonna would perform her tooth magic again if we begged.

"Please, Nonna. Please. Do that thing with your teeth."

Once I was at that phase of the asking, I had already wiggled my way up onto her quintessential grandmother lap. And then I would place my two tiny hands on her cheeks, just below her ear lobes, and turn her face toward mine.

I know now that she was seeing the face of her daughter in my face, and the eyes of the same – eyes that she stared into so deeply, so lovingly, as if recalling the days when her middle child was that young, with hair that dark, and disposition that insistent.

"*Please, Nonna. Please. You haven't done it at all today.*"

Nonna would never answer.

She would just leave me gently hanging, hanging onto the hope that her wizardry would visit soon, and only occasionally relinquishing the most imperceptible flattening of the lips, suggesting she was hiding something.

Hiding her answer.

Hiding her pacing.

Hiding her teeth.

It would never be long before most of the remaining eight grandchildren would make their way to Nonna's side. The burden of the begging became a shared event as it spread from the youngest to the eldest. "*Please Nonna. Please Nonna,*" until there was a united front, a chorus of pre- and post-pubescent offspring chanting the request louder and louder and louder.

And then, as if overcome by the unbalanced ratio of child to adult, she would flash a glimpse to tease us, a turtle from its shell, before her teeth would flee back to their hiding places.

Squeals of laughter would fill the room – until my hands would return to her cheeks, her soft, soft, wrinkled cheeks, and turn her face to my face once more.

"*Please Nonna. That wasn't it. You know that wasn't it.*"

And it was not until it happened that we would know if it would *really* happen. It was never until it unfolded, so rapidly, so unexpectedly and spontaneously, that we would really know.

But when it did, it was as if we had never asked; it was as if we had never waited. Without a hint of warning or a glimmer of having acquiesced, she would magically push her teeth way out of her mouth – way, way out of her mouth, so that they were stretching well beyond the boundaries of her lips.

And there they would rest, suspended, for a second or two, until just as easily, just as unexpectedly and spontaneously, she would pull them back in. Out, in – while her face reddened from the heightened attention and this most uncharacteristic display from this unequivocally ladylike woman.

And like thumbs pulled from a bucket of water, first leaving a depression and then offering no trace, they were gone – as if they had never been.

"Did you see'em? Did you see'em?"

"How do you *do* that, Nonna? How?"

"I missed it. Do it again. *Please* do it again."

But she would stand, instead, shedding grandchildren as she glided away, and walk off quietly to the kitchen – to check on her *ravioli* or to rejoin her daughters and her daughter-in-law. And those of us who still believed would remain in the warmth that her body had left and press our thumbs behind the back of our front teeth, and push, and push, and push.

And push and push.

And push and push.

Until an adult entered to shake a head at us and to call us to the table, where we would spend half of our minutes concentrating on not spilling our milk and the other half staring at our grandmother's teeth, as she chewed her hand-carved *ravioli.*

....

Images of all of us young again, except for Nonna, who remained as old as she always was, are what accompanied me to my pillow that night. Girls with bobbed haircuts and boys with shaved heads. Both with no evidence of the gray that has long enjoyed its view from atop our highest peaks.

The crispness of the evening's breath had turned more aggressive in the hours following sundown and had manifested itself in our own breath, which had taken on a life of its own inside our room. The tall, wooden shutters, that did much to inspire a label of quaint, did little to warm our bodies.

Laurie was wearing thin, cotton, summer pajamas – matching top and bottom. I slept at the other end of the fashion spectrum, in shorts and a tee-shirt. Neither of those outfits, when added to a wool blanket, was enough to slice through the escalating chill of the room.

"I am freezing," Laurie said.

"Me, too."

"I am putting on more clothes," Laurie said.

"Me, too."

We slipped out of our twin beds, touching our cold toes onto the frigid ceramic floor, and tiptoed across to our suitcases to rummage through our belongings for anything that would dull the frigidity. Within a minute or two, we were back under the sheets with various permutations of fleece socks, sweat pants, and turtlenecks covering our bodies.

"Who***oo***o***o***o," shot through our lips as we suffered the wrath of our abandoned beds – retaliating for our having exposed them to the mountain torture. A horizontal bicycle ride under the covers was a friction disappointment, so we moved our heads from the pillows, where our flesh was bared and vulnerable, to the space that loomed just above our knees.

We were locked in a frigid, fetal hell as a silence emerged, a long silence – until a familiar chorus of words rang out.

"I am still freezing."

"Me, too."

"I am getting more clothes."

"Me, too."

Both of us climbed out of bed again, flicked on the light, and ransacked our bags. Laurie threw me a pair of her extra fleece socks, put on another turtleneck, a sweater, and her windbreaker. I put the fleece socks on my hands, pulled on a pair of jeans, crammed the drapes into the slats of the blinds, and yanked a Women's World Cup baseball hat so tightly over my ears that my temples started to invent disco rhythms.

Laurie switched off the light before she immersed herself in sheets and blankets. And then there was silence again. And more silence. And then more.

But it was not the silence of sleepers.

It was the silence of death.

The gradual, unhurried, deliberate march of death.

Until Laurie's bold honesty punctuated the stillness.

"I am still freakin' freezin' over here," Laurie screamed out from under her covers.

"Me, too," I muffled back before bursting into laughter.

We knew we were on an hysteria precipice. Just one centimeter short of going over the edge. Still, the covers flew off, and lights were turned on again. We skidded across the floor like clumsy ballerinas – laughing out loud as Laurie headed for the closet to find two blankets whose combined depth was pale. I ran into the bathroom, looked dreamily at the plastic shower curtain, considered its usefulness, and left the bathroom empty-handed.

We slid underneath the covers, wished that spooning was an option, and raced our legs back and forth like two sticks bent on igniting a spark.

"Are *you* gonna turn off the light?" was heard over the rustle.

"I can't. I can't reach out from under the covers. Are *you*?"

"No. I can't either."

In the brief aftermath of the standoff, another silence, a kind of *new* silence, permeated the room. It was the silence of asthmatic laughter and a complete surrendering to the idiocy of the moment. And the idiocy of our appearance, that caught my eye most clearly then when I glimpsed Laurie, in sixty-three layers of clothing, splashing under the covers like a bass on a sidewalk.

We exploded in laughter. Our fists pounded the mattress, we gasped for breath, and howling permeated the room. A passerby would have slowed to try to unravel the antics behind our door.

The hysteria was better than a wood stove.

Several minutes later, as the tiny ripples of our outbreak moved in the opposite direction of labor pains, further and further apart, we found ourselves shutting down and giving into the power of sleep – either the sleep of emotional and physical fatigue or the sleep of hypothermia. The importance of its origins was swiftly overrun by the deliciousness of the outcome. And with my eyelids fixed heavily, firmly, on top of my eyes, I heard dreamily, in soft waves, with the lights still on, the last words of our first full day.

"I wonder what tomorrow will bring…."

…………

The *comune* (town hall) office had hours that were as fickle and minimal as was possible for a government agency. They opened their doors two days per week for two hours per day.

"Angels," Laurie said, when the sign indicated we were there at just the right time on just a right day. "Angels."

We stopped to soak up the window boxes that decorated the exteriors of the homes that surround the *piazza*. Window boxes that must have been brought inside each night to protect them from their mountain surroundings. Window boxes that were holding fragile petals of nearly all the colors of the rainbow. That were so similar and yet different – each one marking the insiders' attempts to distinguish themselves from their neighbors.

The tall, arched, wooden door to the offices signaled something uncharacteristically official, as did the harsh linoleum floors and the undecorated walls. We had barely passed through the lobby to the waiting area when a poorly-disguised whisper and stare from both parts of an already-seated couple wended their way to our ears and eyes. A broad-toothed smile and a most direct kind of question from the man immediately followed.

"Are you the two foreigners?"

"Yes. We are the two foreigners."

"The two foreigners from America who are looking for their Italian relatives? Campo di Giove relatives?"

"Yes."

Self-congratulatory behavior spread throughout the stale air as he pursed his lips, folded his arms across his chest, and nodded to his wife, as if he had just, in a solitary act of daring and brilliance, broken the genetic code. In reality, a headless person would have been able to mark us as *le due straniere*.

The two foreigners.

Our casual sneakers, jeans, tee-shirts, and hairstyles, or even the pace with which our feet carried us across the linoleum, had placed us in a different world and a different time. We lived and breathed and dressed and behaved in stark contrast to the Italians around us, who, as always, were dressed as if they were headed for an event.

As they were.

The event of the present.

The event of each waking moment.

"Have you had luck so far?" the woman leaned forward to ask.

"We have, thank you. And now we are hoping the town hall will help us even more. But already, just yesterday afternoon, in the documents of *La Chiesa di Sant'Eustachio*, we found our great-grandparents' record of marriage and the baptismal account of our *nonna*."

"Oh," they said as they nodded casually – grotesquely unaware of the significance of those treasures. To them, Campo di Giove may merely be a town in Italy – where they were raised, schooled, and employed. To us, Campo di Giove was folkloric, a mystery, one of the keys to our *nonna's* world and, therefore, our own.

The couple gave us their blessing and stood to shake our hands. It would make good dinner conversation. They could say that they had met *le due straniere* in the town hall, in the town hall, mind you, right before they marched upstairs to continue their research.

As Laurie and I made our way to the second floor offices, we were, admittedly, unaware of just how things would evolve. But we *were* aware of our great fantasy – to find her birth home. To find the home in which *nonna* was born, and then raised, by parents who left Campo di Giove in the latest years of the 19th century, to travel across the Atlantic by ship, to give their children a different kind of life in a different kind of culture.

My mother and I had made the discovery of her father's birth home in the hill town of Tusa in the outskirts of Palermo more than ten years earlier. When the two of us stood outside his house, looking up at the balcony to his room, and later, touching the front door to his youth, my mother dropped to her knees and started to weep. I joined her at her side, on the earth, and felt, so closely, so deeply, the grandfather who had died before I was born. And she felt, so profoundly, the father who had died more than thirty years before as if he had died that very day.

Finding Nonna's birth home was the *primary* hope we harbored when we walked into the office – an office that would either answer or deny.

Two gentlemen looked up from their seats when we first entered. It was the kind of look that cemented their chins to their chests and had their eyes wander high up into their sockets – still leaving room for a kind of scrutiny.

"*Buon giorno*," the elder of the two said.

"*Buon giorno*," we answered.

"May I help you?"

"We hope so…

Smoke filled the agency. Both men dragged from cigarettes as they stepped away from a book they had been studying. They ambled over to the counter, like cowpokes moseying up to a bar with a herd of buffalo perched squarely on their backs. Slowly. Speculatively. Both had their sleeves rolled up to their forearms; the boss was bearded, in grays and blacks, with the mildest hint of cynicism tucked below; the younger was clean-cut, with short hair and the kind of expression that rendered him perpetually shy or embarrassed.

"… This is my cousin, Laura Ragonese, and my name is Marta Ragonese Cummings." The taxi driver in Rome, who questioned my Italian heritage with a *cognome* like Cummings, would be the last on this trip to mistake me.

"We are from the United States and are in search of information about our grandmother, Beatrice Rubeo, who was born in Campo di Giove in March of 1887. We know you are very busy, but we are wondering if you would be so kind as to help us find any documents and any facts about our *nonna's* life here in Campo di Giove."

The boss took a long, hard drag on his cigarette before he spoke again. Then he blew the smoke toward the ceiling and snuffed out the remnants in a glass ashtray that was overflowing with unfiltered chaos.

"Two granddaughters from America in search of their roots? *Brave. Bravissime.* It is important to know where we're from. Or, as we say, we will not know where we're going…

"Eh? Eh?," he continued. And then, before I could even nod my agreement, he said, "Now, tell us what you two think of our little village, our little village of Campo di Giove." And then he reached for another cigarette before he leaned onto the counter with both elbows, resting his chin on his hands.

"To us, it is anything but little, *Signori.* To us, it could not be bigger. We *love* it. The air, the mountains, so extraordinary, and, above all, the people. So friendly. I have traveled from the very north of Italy to the very south, and the people of Campo di Giove are among the kindest I have ever met."

They both smiled and nodded and rolled up their sleeves even farther and confirmed what I had uncovered long ago. That while unsurpassed food, wine, art, architecture, and geography are the hallmarks of the Italian culture, the reigning queen, always and forever, is flattery. I was not surprised, then, when the supervisor said, "OK, *ragazze*, I am Nello, and this is Tonino." And then he took a long drag from his new *sigaretta* and blew white smoke up to the ceiling before adding, "Let us see what we can do for *queste due americane.* Now then, your grandmother, Beatrice Rubeo, eh? Date of birth – March 1887. *Milleottocentottantasette.* Beatrice Rubeo…."

The elder of the two headed straight for a gray filing cabinet with narrow but deep drawers that were filled with hundreds of chronologically-arranged note cards. He continued to repeat my *nonna's* name and birth date as the other opened an unlocked, steel, gray closet with a twist of a silver handle, exposing an array of old books with fraying bindings and broken leather.

The younger moved his fingers along the bindings of the books and would occasionally stop, take one out, look at the front, shake his head, and replace it in the exact same location.

The boss's fingers moved through the cards with ease and authority, like a librarian in a small town, where the old way of doing things lingers. Where, in the battle of the personal touch versus efficiency, most of us who would have to wait a little longer would feel a little better.

The Italian that was exchanged between the two *signori* was rapid as they tried to trace their records for a hint of our grandmother's past. It was different from the Italian I had studied at the *Università Italiana per Stranieri* (Italian University for Foreigners) at Perugia nearly fifteen years before. My three-month course had to focus on the nuts and bolts of the language to guide me to some semblance of fluency in record time. I was less able to dabble in the nuances, the idiomatic nature of speech and culture. So I spoke formally and, more often than not, like an actor in a play who knows her lines but is yet to master the emotion that must accompany them. But the natives, the natives, they sing. And with the kind of spirit that tells the listeners that they not only understand their lines but that they write them and breathe them and live them.

Ah.

There was an urgency to Nello's and Tonino's discourse. A direction. I knew that they wanted to succeed, that they wanted to prove that there was order in their cultural turmoil. That when it came to family, there was no room for carelessness or frivolity.

Questions and suggestions passed from Nello to Tonino and, occasionally, back again, as each worked his fingers through the drawers of the town's history. Our history. I spent my minutes watching their every move or fiddling with the pages of my journal or picking at the skin around my thumbs. The large clock on the wall ticked off the minutes loudly. Chunk. Chunk. Chunk.

I had waited more than thirty years.

I had no idea how tired I was of waiting.

And then Tonino pulled a book from the cabinet, unfolded it in front of his boss's eyes, and placed his pointer finger on the yellowed page. The boss was the first to speak.

"Beatrice Rubeo. Born 16 March 1887. Born to Vincenzo Rubeo and Felicia Candida Fiorinanni. Is that right?"

Nello brought the book to the countertop that separated us from our *nonna's* birth. Each of the men took a side and held it toward *them* – to protect the privacy of others. The fraying binding rested on its heel and the pages opened up into a "V." Their fingers hovered above the markings and traced the details of our *nonna's* birth and gave life to the scene that had happened well over 100 years ago. In Campo di Giove. In Abruzzo.

And when I heard those words, or spoke them as a child, only the letters of the words presented themselves in my imagination. Black letters rising up and down against the white screen of my mind. No images. No sense that Campo di Giove was a real place with real people that still thrived after my grandmother had left. It was only my nonna who was real. They were just letters dancing in my head.

And then my nonna died...

And I wondered where Campo di Giove was.

"Yes," I said, as my eyes filled with tears, "that is right. You have found her."

Laurie's hands and mine were locked in an impenetrable grip – a grip of enchantment and disbelief. Her eyes were filled, as well, and my body ached. I felt tired and trapped between the celebration of Nonna's birth and the reliving of her death, between the childhood exuberance that sometimes kisses adulthood and the death of a grandparent that ends our youth.

The two men looked at us and were every bit a part of our emotion. And while the mystique and reality of the American Dream could not be denied, what could be denied is its ability to answer *all* our dreams.

It was, after all, a rectangular office in a small town *comune*, surrounded by window boxes, hand-carved wooden doors, cool alpine breezes, and trusting natives, that fulfilled one of my biggest dreams and provided the pages on which was scrawled the birth of the grandmother who performed magic. Who was magic.

As Tonino moved for a box of tissues, my hand moved over my mouth, and my feet took me backwards to a place against the wall. Nello nodded at me, as if to ask permission to move on. And he did, as he began to sing out words that graced the pages of her arrival. The words that had not been uncovered, ever, never, by those who had begun life on "the other side." And there we were, in Campo di Giove, cooled by the shadows of a shelter – the shelter of those words.

Felicia, the mother of our grandmother, was nicknamed Lucia and made wool clothes. Vincenzo was six years older than his twenty-one year-old wife when he got married. He was the head of a farming agency – a *capo*. Business had drawn him out of town when our *nonna*, his second daughter, was delivered at her own home by an *ostretrica* – a midwife, named Teresa Colarossi. Because of our great grandfather's absence, two other natives of Campo di Giove bore witness to the birth of our grandmother. Those witnesses fixed their signatures onto my *nonna's* birth page with the script of another era and confirmed the healthy, beautiful entrance into this town, this country, this world, of Beatrice Rubeo on 16 March 1887.

The witnesses' names…

Palumbo Donato. Antonetti Francesco.

"Oh, my God," I said out loud. "Oh, my God."

My words were spoken in English, but Nello and Tonino needed no translation.

Antonetti Francesco

The witness to my grandmother's birth.

My mouth was surely open when I asked Laurie if she thought that it was possible. If what we were seeing could possibly mean something else.

"It must be. It has to be...

"My mother…" I said as I turned to the two men who so gently, so patiently, held the witnesses in their arms. "My mother's name is Antonietta Francesca – Antoinette Frances back home. I am wondering, now, I am wondering if she was named after the witness to her mother's birth."

"Ahh," they both said as they nodded. "It is possible," Nello continued. "The names are reversed in Italy, but they are the same roots, *piccola*." I smiled as he called me "little one."

"I was named Antoinette after my father's mother," my mother used to say. "But I don't know where the Frances came from. And I never asked my mother. It was one of many things I never asked."

"What else, Mum? What else do you wish you had asked her?"

"Too many things. More about Campo di Giove. How her mother and sisters lived while my nonno was in America preparing for them to come. From where their ship to America left and how they got there. The ship ride. Who met them at Ellis Island. Where they first went. Why they settled in Milford. Too many questions. Too many things to think about. Just ask me all your questions now, dear. Don't let it happen again. Ask me all your questions now."

"There is more," Nello said in the middle of my wanderings. "Shall I continue?"

"*Si, si, prego.*"

I was back up to the counter then, leaning against it with both hands, arms taut, one hand gripping a tissue that Tonino had offered. My eyes were steaming, searing from the tears that had been repressed as well as those that had pushed their way through.

I knew, again, that I could never explain my emotion – the emotion I feel when I am there, in Italy. It starts the moment my feet touch the soil, and it starts in the center of my soul, of my spirit, and dances. Skips. And lives with abandon, until it unhinges itself and works its way up, up to my eyes, my speech, my cheeks, my walk, my attitude, in a way that it *never* does anywhere else.

Our great-grandparents' wedding record.

Our grandmother's baptismal document.

A touch of her baptismal font.

Their baptismal font.

Our *nonna's* birth certificate.

Details about her parents' occupations.

The ages they were when they were married.

The midwife who delivered my grandmother in her home.

The witnesses to her birth…

"Your *nonna* was born at 8:20 PM," Nello said, "and as I mentioned, at her own home. Her home on Via Forno Vecchio, 9."

"*Come?*"

"Via Forno Vecchio. *Numero nove.*"

My chest started to move up and down then. The address. He knew the address. Nello's hand reached across the counter to cover my own. I turned my head toward Laurie then to make sure she knew the news. She just shook her head, back and forth, and back and forth. Tears pooled in her eyes. Tonino reached for *her* hand.

"It says that there? It says the street where she was born?"

"It does."

"Do you know where it is?" I asked.

"*Si*," Tonino said quickly. "It is a very old street in the oldest part of town. It is no longer labeled, and the street itself is covered with vines and grass. But it is still there.

"When you get closer to it, you may want to ask one of our elderly residents to direct you to the exact location. They will remember. They remember it all."

We embraced the hands of Nello and Tonino when we left, nearly two hours after we had entered. Their country, their village, their small town, had come through for us, and we could see their pride in how they smiled and brought dimples to their cheeks.

When Laurie and I moved away from their office and toward the birth home of our grandmother, I turned back to find Nello lighting another cigarette and returning to what he had been doing when we first entered. Tonino was replacing the stack of books that he had unsealed for our eyes – the stack of books that had not only led to the nuances of our grandmother's generation and her parents' generation, but also their parents and their parents.

New names, that were old names, were entered into our family tree: Crescenzo Rubeo and Chiara Palumbo – the parents of *nonna's* father; Eliodoro Fiorinanni and Anna Crispina de Chellis – the parents of *nonna's* mother; Matteo Rubeo and Anna Lucia Palumbo – the parents of the parents of *nonna's* father. And new occupations: a *sarta* (seamstress), a *calzolaio* (shoemaker), and a *casalinga* (housewife). In America, *nonna* had become a wonderful *sarta*. And she married a man who, for a time, sold shoes.

We kept turning the pages, backwards in time, until there were no longer any pages to turn, or until the years or the elements had weathered them beyond recognition. The page of Matteo Rubeo, my great-great-grandfather, was torn – spoiled by moisture and almost too fragile to be unfolded for our generation to see.

At that point we, too, were too fragile, and I was grateful, on some level, for the end of the road.

....

The road to *nonna's* street sloped upward, and it pulled us toward the oldest part of the city – where buildings were uninhabited, parts of the stone had turned to dust, windows were sealed over with cement, and frames were kept from crumbling by ancient wooden beams.

We found our way to one lane that was abandoned under the deep blue skies of Abruzzo – where gentle daytime breezes escorted fresh air down from the mountaintops and into our path. Mounds of earth and unwieldy vegetation spanned the alley's breadth. Shreds of splintered cement skidded beneath our shoes as we tangled ourselves in roots and disturbed the villages of European insects.

Our hands and eyes searched for names and numbers, street signs and house details, but the ceramic tiles had long-since faded or the etchings had grown softer or the numbers moved in strange patterns, from 3 to 14 to 7A. We dug through the grooves of the etchings to expose the details that had been hidden for years. Still, no *numero nove*.

We hiked the length of the land and uncovered half-moon decorations, small holes in the façades where rods had been inserted to prevent a collapse, and waves of ivy that had sprawled in every direction since forever. I found a tiny, glass bottle, filled with dirt and completely unmarked. Unremarkable, except for the fact that I may have unburied it from under my *nonna's* old street.

We picked up building shards and tucked them into our packs.

We went about our task like two archaeologists on a mission of discovery. Both of us void of emotion. Perhaps because we were already spent or perhaps because we were not sure we were on the right street.

We had no more tears to waste.

Laurie and I finally left the lane in search of elderly advice, but only after barely evading a gaping hole that was masked by a grassy covering. Laurie found the hole not by stepping into it, which would have plunged her at least thirty feet below the surface of the earth, but by stepping to the side, for no apparent reason, and later bending over to push the grass away to scour the ground, for no apparent reason.

…………

Iolanda, who had been affectionately (and privately) dubbed Yo and then Yo Yo and then Yo Yo Ma, responded to our knock on the door of her 16th century home with a clap of her hands, an enormous smile, two warm hugs, and an immediate and glorious invitation to lunch. We had just traveled back nearly 200 years, and we were ravenous and completely unfulfilled by our hotel's breakfast fare of melba squares and strawberry jam.

Still, lunch was an hour or so away. So, as the veal squares with tomatoes, potatoes, and a heavenly array of spices simmered on Yo Yo's glistening stainless steel stove, the three of us agreed to head for the local *cimitero* – cemetery, to continue to uncover our family history.

The walk to the cemetery was familiar then – down the same sloping street that had taken us to *La Chiesa di Sant'Eustachio*, but then just to the right of the old church to a much wider road that welcomes the procession of tourists in the height of the season.

The road was empty – except for three cousins, one nearing seventy and two in their forties, who spanned the dimensions of height to such a degree that no one could have imagined they were related. Iolanda had explained, in the first few minutes of our first visit, the reasons for her relative shortness in a branch of the family that leaned more toward tall than small. It had happened on the steps of her childhood home.

She was only a nine year-old when she slipped on the stone stairs leading away from her back door. She fell hard and tumbled downward, head over heels, and ended up at the bottom of the unforgiving *scale*, with many fractured bones in her back.

The doctor was unskilled, she said, and unaware of how to save her from never growing another inch in her torso for the rest of her life.

"Look at my feet," she said. "They are big…

"Look at my legs," she said. "They are long…

"I would have been tall if he had known what he was doing." Her face reddened then, with embarrassment and anger, as if it had happened yesterday.

The cemetery was gated but open. It was Laurie's first visit to an Italian graveyard where, since burial in the ground is viewed as something of a disgrace, mausoleums and crypts abound, and black and white photographs of the deceased are mounted on the outside of the marble or granite in oval frames. Although startling at first, in the end the photographs bring personality to the etchings of names and dates and epitaphs. They bring a sense of life and awareness that this was someone's daughter or son or mother or uncle or sister – dressed in their finest cravats, pearls, or wool suits, staring off to the side, sternly, humorlessly.

Their seriousness used to haunt me, but now I am convinced that a smiling face on a tombstone would haunt me more.

The three of us walked together through the cemetery grounds. The breezes of the morning were gone then, and the uninterrupted sun bore down on us, presenting such a stark contrast to the frigidity of the evening before. The earth was dry, arid, and made a scraping sound under our feet.

Iolanda pointed out the tombs of her family members from another branch and turned when tears visited her eyes. Laurie and I were in search of our own family members – those members of the Fiorinanni Family or the Rubeo Family who never, ever left.

We visited each tomb and stretched our necks from the very tops of the sites to the very bottoms. With relentless precision and patience, we stepped quietly and respectfully from one stone to the next. A handful of workers in the rear of the *cimitero* watched us in-between the movements of their chisels, as they worked their way through the thickness of the stone.

With each turn, we had renewed anticipation.

And hope.

And then disappointment.

I saw the tomb of an Antonetti Francesco – born the same year as my grandmother. I wondered if he were the son or the son of the son of the witness to my *nonna's* birth.

And then more hope.

And more disappointment.

In the end, when the futility of our task was clear, Iolanda told the story of the wartime decree – that families whose deceased did not yet have tombs would be thrown into a mass grave underneath the cemetery office. She knew before we stepped through those gates that there was not a trace of a Fiorinanni or a Rubeo inside. But she had allowed us to carry our hope with us, so that we could answer the question for ourselves and not hold her responsible for the news of their absence.

She then asked if we wanted to see what lay underneath before she walked us over. We bent low to see through the bars into the makeshift burial below the ground. The remnants were tossed. Skeletal heads, arms, legs, and ribs, scattered in disheveled patterns.

I spoke quietly over the collection and wondered if those whose births we had just celebrated in the *comune* were below us then in a burial that was anything but celebratory.

Matteo Rubeo and Anna Lucia Palumbo
Crescenzo Rubeo and Chiara Palumbo
Eliodoro Fiorinanni and Anna Crispina de Chellis

Minutes later, we left through the wrought-iron gate. Iolanda's long legs kept pace with us as we moved slowly away from the cemetery and back toward the heart of Campo di Giove. I welcomed the shade of *La Chiesa di Sant'Eustachio* and its baptismal font – which was, again, cool to the touch, even though we passed by without entering.

Chapter Four

ANGELS
Campo di Giove, Abruzzo

Iolanda's phone was ringing as she was inserting the key into her back door. She raced to answer it, and I heard her describing and then defending the whirlwind of activity since the evening before.

"Yes, two Americans.

"Yes, relatives.

"Their *bisnonno* and your *bisnonna* were brother and sister.

"Yes, it was your husband who led them to me, Filomena.

"Well, there wasn't much time.

"We are about to sit down for lunch. But after that, yes, of course. Yes, of course your father. Lina and Serena, too."

The prizes in Iolanda's possession for the past two days were finally to be shared and displayed for all to see. The wave of our arrival had found its way to those with an equal claim to our roots. I knew the cavalcade of relatives was imminent. But in a gesture that confirmed, more than anything else, the link between the Campo di Giove family and the American family, first, first, first and above all, we would sit down to eat. Everything, including 100 years in search of a common blood, across mountains, oceans, and the chasms of different cultures, could wait for food.

Everything.

The lunch table was prepared with accuracy and class. Dusted and then covered with a linen tablecloth that was immediately removed because of a faint spot near the edge. Another was unfolded, secured, and quickly decorated with china, crystal, silver, and linen napkins.

Iolanda then began the march of delicacies. Veal squares with potatoes and tomatoes. Lettuce tossed only with olive oil and salt. Wine, water, and *Fanta* to drink. And fresh *mozzarella.*

"Argilla, Argilla!" Iolanda had yelled from the street after we had passed by *La Chiesa di Sant'Eustachio* on our walk home from the cemetery. "Argilla! *Ho bisogno di mozzarella fresca!* I need fresh *mozzarella*."

Argilla's husband dropped his rake after proper introductions and cupped his hands around his mouth before he echoed Iolanda's words.

"Argilla! Argilla! Iolanda *needs* fresh *mozzarella*!"

Argilla pushed through the front door with an immediacy that suggested she had been expecting us and whisked her way outside her fence.

"Argilla," Iolanda began. "These are my two cousins from…"

"Yes, I know," she interrupted. "I ran into some people who had been to the town hall this morning. They met your cousins in the lobby there.

"So," Argilla continued as she turned to us. "Welcome to Campo di Giove. What do you think of Abruzzo? I have relatives in the United States. They live near New York. You know New York? Do you live near there? You need fresh *mozzarella*, eh? Fresh, fresh *mozzarella*. Follow me. Follow me to the best *mozzarella* in Italia."

Through the streets of Campo di Giove Laurie and I traipsed, like sheep, without an original thought or any will to influence our own direction. The speed of Argilla's speech kept pace with her feet. Iolanda only broke into their dialogue to point out the homes of her relatives – a brother, a niece, and a great nephew – cushioned in relatively new condominiums at the foothills of the local mountains.

Argilla unlocked the door to her family's *mozzarella* factory, secured a kerchief around her hair, and disappeared into the back room. In the front, we were surrounded by stainless steel equipment, polished with exactitude. I could see my reflection in the machinery and was shamed by my informality – my jeans and sweatshirt. Dirt from the cemetery was still on my boots.

As I was reaching down to dust them off, Argilla emerged with several balls of *mozzarella fresca* floating in milky water. "These were just finished this morning. They will be very good. Very, very good. You will see."

"They will be," Iolanda said. "This is, without question, the best."

As the container made its way from Argilla's hands to Iolanda's, I examined and compared its contents with another cheese of my dreams. *Parmigiano*.

Parmigiano, I thought, in solid form, is only for the brave – for those who dare to hold a square firmly in the hand, bring it to the lips, and then bite, resolutely, into the heart of the chunk. Once inside, the cheese consumes the mouth, bouncing off every active taste bud and awakening those that had been forever dormant.

The tasting of the *parmigiano* is, however, a private party – one that is enjoyed by only the consumer and is feared by surrounding company. Its odor is piercing, omnipotent – taking no prisoners, clearing a room – leaving only the chewer, with her tongue and taste buds, in a solitary state of euphoria as she reaches for a glass of *vino rosso* to punctuate the era of bliss.

Mozzarella, on the other hand, is for those who do not want to wage a battle. No bravery is required – only a quiet moment, when the *mozzarella* can be delicately splintered into thin circles or even swallowed whole. *Mozzarella* scares away no one and even invites guests into its range of influence – fresh tomatoes, *basilico*, olive oil. It travels to the tongue, the taste buds, even the roof of the mouth, and delights in putting everything back to sleep. Not a dull sleep, but the sleep of heaven.

As Yo Yo Ma escorted the *mozzarella* to the dining room table, I felt inspired by Argilla's and her declaration that this would be the best *mozzarella* in all of Italia. And I felt a sense of urgency.

So right after the cheese sculptures came to rest just under my nose and Iolanda turned her back to extinguish the stove's flame, I flashed my fingers toward the array, promptly skidded the tiniest *mozzarella* ball across a dribble of olive oil, and popped it, in its entirety, into my mouth. When Yo Yo turned back from the burner, the *mozzarella* remained steady and motionless in my mouth. Whole, but slowly melting. Circumstantial evidence rested at the corners of my lips in the shape of olive oil, as my teeth slowly, surreptitiously, worked the cheese within its confines.

"Please begin," Iolanda said, moving toward me with a spoon in hand. "*Prego*, help yourself. But before we begin, Marta, please, do me the honor of a blessing."

Dear Lord.

The succulence of the moment and the wad still pressed inside my mouth precluded me from uttering even a mere "*grazie*," never mind a religious blessing. The cheese was melting into every nook of my mouth and was usurping, little by little, control of my breathing. My deliberations. The *mozzarella* of home would feel disgraced in this company of flawlessness – a flawlessness that had the right to condescend, to ridicule, to spurn, although its gentle grace would never allow it such cruelty.

"Oh!" Iolanda cried out, spinning at once with spoon in hand to return to her kitchen. "I forgot the bread! *Dio, Dio.*"

So with her back to our table, and with her arms working methodically to change a mass of bread into thick slices, I chewed. And chewed and chewed, until the last morsel of *mozzarella* and my mouth parted company. And I could speak again. "Oh, my God, Lau'," I whispered. "You've *got* to taste the *mozzarella.*"

"Already did," she said.

"You did? When?"

"I grabbed one right after you did. I couldn't wait."

"Can you stand it?"

"This is the best *mozzarella* I have ever had."

"Do you love this country or what?"

"Do you love *Iolanda* or what?"

We were smiling when Iolanda made her way back to the table with the bread arranged haphazardly on a cutting board.

"OK, Marta, Laura," Iolanda sang out as she placed the fresh *pane* on the dining room table right next to the *mozzarella*, "we are finally ready. But before we begin, we must say grace. Marta, *ti prego.*"

So I stood, reaching for the hand of my elder cousin on my left and my other on my right, first delivering our childhood "Bless us oh, Lord..." before breaking into a more casual unction.

"Yo Yo Ma has prepared us a meal,
Lots of veggies and spice tossed with veal,
The repast will be swell,
'Cos of the mozzarell',
This we know 'cos of those we did steal.
Amen."

I was grateful throughout my little offering for the power of language – for the opportunity it allowed me to be able to speak in

English for a moment and to have a laugh. For allowing me to talk without thinking and with a brand of humor that Laurie might appreciate but that might get lost in the translation.

But then I noticed that *Iolanda* was laughing.

At precisely the right moment.

And to the exact right degree.

And then she picked up her spoon, slowly scooped up three balls of *mozzarella*, one at a time, and placed them down on my plate with an omniscience that was subtle.

And then, in broken but perfectly suitable British, Iolanda said, "Marta, did you know you've still a bit of olive oil on your lips?"

Pasquale, Iolanda's brother, entered the dining room as we were clearing away dessert – juicy, rich peaches that Iolanda had long ago pealed and jarred with just water and sugar before she had set them aside to mature. The peaches were as soothing to my mouth as Pasquale was to my eyes.

He was a tall gentleman, *a gentleman*, with gray hair, a thin countenance and frame. He was dressed in a light blue, sharply-pressed, cotton, button-down shirt, a dark-blue vest, and a tweed sports jacket with gray slacks. His daughter, Filomena, whose coloring and shape of face linked her to her father in unmistakable ways, followed him into the room. Her hair was neatly-styled, with hints of gray at the temples. She wore a brightly-colored skirt, a white cotton shirt that was enhanced by a long gold chain, and a sweater, with an occasional thin stripe – one of which was a precise match for the color of her skirt. Her shoes, like her father's, were leather and ideal complements to the rest of her attire.

Laurie and I rose to go to their sides – first to Pasquale's and then to Filomena's. There had been little to no explanation of who they were, but Iolanda had offered enough over the course of our two meetings to decode the holes. Pasquale and my mother were second cousins. Pasquale's grandmother and my mother's grandfather were sister and brother. The latter went to America, the former stayed in Campo di Giove. Filomena was Laurie's and my third cousin. Those same siblings were our great-grandparents.

Pasquale's hands were soft to the touch, as were Filomena's. They were a study in Italian posturing – cautious, careful on the outside, unparalleled warmth on the inside. I knew this already from the way they took our hands, looked deeply into our eyes, and welcomed us into their family within moments of their arrival.

Our arrival.

Still, there was a hint of formality in the room, even an exotic aura, as we stared at and into their cages, and they stared into ours.

At first blush, our exteriors seemed dramatically different, though I could see some link in our complexions. The pales and light browns of my brother Anthony and my sister Cindy were staring back at me. But Pasquale, Iolanda, and Filomena were sculpted by a European past, and we were sculpted by a much briefer American experience.

It showed in their clothing. It showed in our clothing. It showed in the ways we all carried ourselves, in how we laughed, smiled, moved, spoke, used our hands, and listened.

We were strangers.

But we were family.

Pasquale seated himself at the head of the table and beckoned us to join him. Filomena offered to stand so that we might sit. When we resisted, we received the kind of Italian reprimand that makes one realize there is no room for negotiating. The battle had already been decided. The war was over.

Laurie and I sat down. Iolanda did, too. Filomena stood beside the dining room table and turned to listen to her father when he began to speak. He had a brand of Italian that was a bit harder to decipher as it hid itself inside his mouth; his lips gave few clues of the sounds to follow. When he talked, his mouth made a perfect "O," and everyone in the room listened.

In short order, I knew that his ninety year-old mind was as sharp as if he were twenty. It was with remarkable clarity that he filled in some blanks of the family tree – that my great-grandfather, Vincenzo Rubeo, and Pasquale's grandmother, Lucia Rubeo, had two other siblings – Francesco and Matteo. Francesco had gone to the United States with Vincenzo. We were then sure that Campo di Giove cousins flourished in the United States – in places none of us knew about, with faces we had never met.

Like Iolanda, he spoke of his father, Paolino Capaldo, who had gone to the United States, but had come back.

Paolino Capaldo.

The owner of the dictionary in the adjoining room.

Iolanda got up from the table and returned with the book. She placed it in front of me, and they watched as Laurie and I leafed through the tattered pages to glimpse English from "the other side."

The silence in the room was thick.

"This dictionary and an old photograph of my father," Iolanda began, ever so slowly, in *italiano*, "these were the only things left after the Germans came to Campo di Giove." Her face reddened then, and her voice lost its liveliness. She sounded tight. Tense. Her eyes stared right at me and through me to the mountains in the distance. "We were eating dinner," she continued. "Right here. In this dining room. We were eating *gnocchi* when there was a loud pounding on the door. When one of us went to open it, the Germans barged in with guns and sticks. They screamed at us and spit on us and began to destroy our house right in front of our eyes.

"They smashed photographs, broke windows, crushed a beautiful chandelier that hung right over our dining room table. Not this table. This is not the same table. They turned that one onto its side. Glass, china, and silver were shattering everywhere. And then they told us that we had to leave the house immediately.

"It was 11 November 1943. The 11th day of the 11th month. I will never forget it. We had to get up from the dining room table, take nothing, and leave the house immediately. Just like that.

"They burst through the door," she said as her voice trailed away, and her eyes moved from the mountains to the faces of her brother and her niece and then to Laurie and me. "They burst through the door, and they changed our lives forever."

Pasquale had his head bent down toward the table, listening to every word his sister had uttered, with a sobriety that suggested the images had not faded in the past fifty-six years.

And then he spoke.

"My wife Carmela was pregnant at the time – with our daughter, Filomena. Carmela was in the last stages of her pregnancy." I turned to Filomena who looked at me and nodded, and then turned back to her father, who continued speaking. "When we left our home in Campo di Giove, we started to walk with nothing but the shirts on our backs. We were cold. We were hungry. Just outside of town, we set up a temporary camp in the woods for my wife to get some rest and some peace. Our plan was to sleep there that night and then begin to walk to Sulmona in the morning – which is several kilometers away.

"We tried our best to sleep that night, because we knew that the next day and the next, we would walk and walk through the mountains and forests of Abruzzo. In time, we walked to the outskirts of Sulmona, to a little town called Porta Pacentrana. There we stopped because my wife was having labor pains. It was early for her to deliver, but the stress of events had set everything in motion.

"We were taken in by an elderly woman named Annina La Melogna. We stayed there until the moment for Carmela to give birth arrived. That moment was on 27 November 1943, sixteen days after we had been forced to flee from Campo di Giove.

"My wife's pain was so strong, so strong that night, we were sure it was time. We knew we had to call on a midwife for help – but the German soldiers occupied that area as well, and I needed permission to make such a call. At first I hesitated. There was a curfew, a strict curfew, and I was afraid to challenge it. Even so, I left the house and ran to the town square on my way to the home of the *ostretrica*.

"There, in the main *piazza*, I was stopped and surrounded by a group of German soldiers armed with machine guns. Their enmity, their weapons, their orders, our cultures, placed me completely at their mercy. And my family's future rested solely on the choices those soldiers would make that evening.

"I explained the situation as best I could, without allowing my nervousness to surface for them to see and ridicule. So I spoke of my wife's pain and the urgency of the instant – hoping to appeal to their senses for the little child who was waiting to be born. And then I waited for their response.

"There was little discussion between the young soldiers. Little disagreement, I supposed. For miraculously, within seconds of my arrival, they let me pass through."

And then Pasquale paused and glanced at his daughter and his sister before continuing. And then he looked at me.

"In the midst of such hatred, there was a moment of kindness. One moment of kindness – and in that window of opportunity, my wife gave birth, and little Filomena was born, in the outskirts of Sulmona, in the middle of the night."

"When we returned," Iolanda said, "not until several months later, near the end of May, 1944, the inside of our house was destroyed. They had ransacked everything. Furniture was ruined. Food we had canned from working the earth was stolen. Even our animals were taken from us. The only things we could find of what we once had were that dictionary in your hands and this photograph of our father. They were both outside, lying under hills of rocks and glass.

"But we rebuilt this house," Iolanda said willfully, remembering their determination and spite. "Step-by-step, we rebuilt this home to what it was before November, 1943. Stone-by-stone. Window-by-window."

I was quiet.

Silent.

I knew my words would sound too simple.

Too distant.

Too privileged.

"This is why people fled Italy for America," Pasquale said before I had to speak. "Long before those things unfolded, some people knew that it would come to that one day."

Filomena walked up behind her father then and placed her hands on his shoulders. She had decided that that was enough. That her father should not spend too many of his remaining minutes reliving the worst elements of that time. So as if to redirect, without being too obvious, she did what, I imagined, she had done so many, many times before.

"*Papa, canta quella canzone per Marta e Laura – la canzone di Mussolini. Conosci la canzone, Papa?*"

"Ah," Pasquale said, inspiring a shift in his demeanor and a smile from his adoring daughter. "The Mussolini song. Yes. I will sing that for them. That, *mia figlia*, is a good idea."

So Pasquale turned toward me at the opposite end and blushed a bit before he began his song – tapping his long, aged fingers on the cloth that protected the mahogany table, that rested under a new chandelier.

È arrivato il momento di sciogliere la matassa
A chi non prende moglie dovrà pagar la tassa
La tassa pagheremo a gran velocità
Grideremo viva la tassa e chi la fa pagar.

Allora le ragazze tutte contente saranno
Evviva il nostro Duce in coro canteranno
Marito trovan tutte o che felicità
Grideremo viva la tassa e chi la fa pagar.

Ci sono in Italia parecchi milioni
Non vogliono prender moglie per non aver pensieri
Non vogliono prender moglie per non aver pensier
La moglie dell'amico se la godono con piacer.

When he finished, he looked up at me with lingering reddened cheeks, and then threw his head back in laughter. It was the unabashed gesture of a small child. And he watched as the rest of the room filled with levity.

"What does it mean?" Laurie asked.

"Well, it begins rather poetically," I said. "'The moment to unravel the skein has come…' But then it changes pretty quickly," I said laughing. "Basically, any man who is not going to marry has to pay a tax. All the women are happy because they think the men will be unwilling to pay the tax – so they are certain this will find them husbands and happiness. They shout 'hooray' for Mussolini, the one who makes them pay the tariff. All the men are happy to run out and *pay* the tax, however, to avoid getting married. They, too, shout 'hooray' for *Il Duce*. In the end, it says that many millions in Italy avoid marriage altogether so they won't have any worries. Instead, they enjoy themselves with their friend's wife!"

"Lovely, eh?" Laurie and I said to each other smiling.

And then we all laughed, and shook our heads…

Until Iolanda got up from the table to return the dictionary to the extra bedroom and to prepare some *caffè*. "But they were tough times," we heard her say as she walked away. "Tough times. We had nothing but the shirts on our backs. Nothing. And now all we have is this dictionary. And the photo. I will never forget that day. I will never forget that day as long as I live."

Pasquale was nodding, agreeing, from his position far away. And as I watched his head move back and forth, still, still in disbelief, and watched Iolanda's dress drift gently over the backs of her knees, and watched Filomena, now in her mid-fifties, relive the stories of the earliest moments of her life, in the cold forest outside of Sulmona, I knew, I knew, that I could never explain to anyone what had just been explained to me.

The power of language, I thought, as the *espresso* waited to boil on the stove. And the fallibility of it, as well.

I sighed and tried to muster the strength to share with Laurie what I had heard and in the manner in which I had heard it. I yearned for her to participate completely in their words, their pasts, their version of their history. But I knew I never could. I knew I could never find that kind of strength. And I knew, then, that I could never guarantee another person's full understanding of a moment – particularly when I could not guarantee my own.

A knock on the door at just that instant startled us a bit, but when it swung open and the looks of Pasquale, Iolanda, and Filomena softened to the greatest degree, we knew that the parade of family was entering its next phase.

Lina, daughter of Filomena.

Serena, daughter of Lina.

Four generations of Campo di Giove had gathered.

Lina had a mix of blonde and brown hair. She was the first of the females in the family, besides *le due americane*, to be wearing something more casual. Brown pants tapered to the heel, a brown shirt, and a tan sweater with a hood that was left unzipped. Her flat leather shoes altogether made an expert match.

Her daughter, Serena, had the hair color of her mother and the face of an angel. Pale with rosy cheeks. Thin lips flattened simply when she smiled. Hands folded across her front when she listened to the adults. She wore sweatpants, sneakers, a Champion sweatshirt, and a plastic watch with bright, bold colors. She had a ring on her right hand, matching earrings, and round glasses.

To the degree that Pasquale and Iolanda were symbols of an old Italy, Serena was a symbol of the new Italy. She could be inserted into a second grade classroom in small town America and go unnoticed. Pasquale and Iolanda, on the other hand, could stroll the streets of that same town and pull the people from their stores and homes and farming to catch a glimpse of something quite different, something from another time.

Serena's mountains of Abruzzo were no longer all that far from Rome and from more distant influences, way across the Atlantic. Pasquale's and Iolanda's mountains were a lifetime away – by foot, by ship, by ideology.

We had not even begun to adjust to the new arrivals when there was another knock on the door. The woman who entered, dressed all in black from head to toe, was my mother's twin. Same height (perpetually-shrinking). Similar shape. Same hair color (salt and pepper). Same hairstyle (short, resting lazily against her head). Same tone and presentation. Again, there was little hint of her link to this scene – just introductions, handshakes, respectful smiles, and tinges of embarrassment.

"This is my cousin Adelina," Iolanda finally said.

"So does that make us cousins, too?" I asked.

"Yes," Adelina responded quickly and matter-of-factly. "I had the same *nonna*, Lucia Rubeo, as Pasquale and Iolanda. Their father Paolino and my mother Filomena were brother and sister. So, just as your mother, Marta, and your father, Laura, are second cousins to Pasquale and Iolanda, I, too, am a second cousin."

The details were causing my head to spin. So many new names. Too many names that ended in *ena* or *ina*. Serena. Lina. Filomena. Adelina. I was equally dizzied by the fact that the subtleties of our family history had already been conveyed to Adelina since our arrival just twenty-four hours ago – over the phone or over the gossip vines. While we were strolling the streets of Campo di Giove, we were unknowingly being explored, and Adelina had been doing her research. She came prepared.

She also came with information about the *casa di Rubeo.*

The house of Rubeo, she called it.

She knew Via Forno Vecchio.

She knew where the home of her grandmother and our great-grandfather still is.

"I can take you there," she said.

"You can?"

"*Si, posso*."

"When?"

"Now."

"*Adesso*?"

"If you would like."

"Yes, we would like."

And so it was that the Family Rubeo collected itself, so immediately, so uniformly, and left Iolanda's home, with the elders in the forefront, marching their way down the steep steps leading away from Iolanda's back door. And then under decaying, ancient archways, past the wooden door-carvings of the old city center, alongside window boxes with flowers that continued to resist the move toward colder days, over largely unvisited terrain, below beams that had fallen down between parallel rows of houses, toward the house of Rubeo.

Together we were a procession. Serena. Lina, Serena's mother. Filomena, Lina's mother. Pasquale, Filomena's father. Iolanda, Pasquale's sister. Adelina, Pasquale's and Iolanda's first cousin. And Laura and Marta.

"We are going to the house where our grandmother was born?"

"Yes, Marta, we are going to the house where your grandmother was born. But this is also the house where your grandmother's *father* was born."

"Does anyone still live there?"

"No, it is abandoned."

And so, with mounting anticipation, we trudged through Campo di Giove – picking up an occasional resident along the way. A very old gentleman who was happy to reminisce. A town historian who was able to comment on the historical nuances of the houses we passed. Two young boys who smiled adorably at us, said "hello," first in *italiano* and then in *inglese*, dropped their bikes, and tagged along for a bit.

But by the time we reached the house, our group was family only.

Adelina's arm lifted up from her side, slowly, with the black material of her mourning floating down from her elbow. Then she pointed to a home of stone, particularly near to where Laurie and I had been earlier. It was marked by a wrought-iron lamplight and one small window that had been cemented shut. The door was a large rectangular opening, several feet off the ground, too high to be entered from earth. The steps from its base had long since worn away, leaving a stiff jump from the entrance to the ground. The door itself was made of old wood – two vertical panels, each of which held five square elements of its own.

Laurie and I stood in front of the house. And stared.

Our mouths were agape. We were exhausted.

Occasionally, we looked at each other.

And shook our heads, again.

Until we heard the utterance of Adelina.

"*Marta, Laura, quest'è la casa di Rubeo. La casa di Rubeo.*"

With her words, tears were ignited, as if by a switch. First off. And then on. Forever nourished by the sounds of Adelina in Italian song – brevity, simplicity, beauty.

La casa di Rubeo.

My throat began to clamp and my body, from its center outward, weakened. Amorphous images of my *nonna* were crossing in my head – from the old, Italian grandmother with the white hair and the magic tricks to the imagined pictures of her as *una bambina*, a baby, born in the house in front of which we were standing. Before a witness named Antonetti Francesco and to parents who made wool clothes and worked the fields of Campo di Giove and beyond.

The house where my grandmother, my *nonna*, was born.

And her father Vincenzo and his sister Lucia, the matriarch of those who surrounded us, of those who had led us to this place.

Our relatives were quiet and were stunned by our tears. I could feel their eyes as our eyes moved along every corner of the *casa*. I knew that they were beginning to understand that *famiglia e radici*, family and roots, had not lost their way on "the other side," had not drowned on the Atlantic journey of 100 years ago.

They did not speak a word until we were ready.

We were not ready for a long time.

When we finally did speak, all we could utter was a "*grazie*." They shook their heads and said it was nothing. And placed their hands on our shoulders and squeezed our flesh between their fingers.

And several minutes later, when we turned to walk away from *la casa di Rubeo*, arms were wrapped around waists, hands pulled shoulders closer together, and wet cheeks met the kisses of a more stoic exterior.

And I knew I would be back.

To stand in the shadows of the home of my *nonna*.

With family.

With friends.

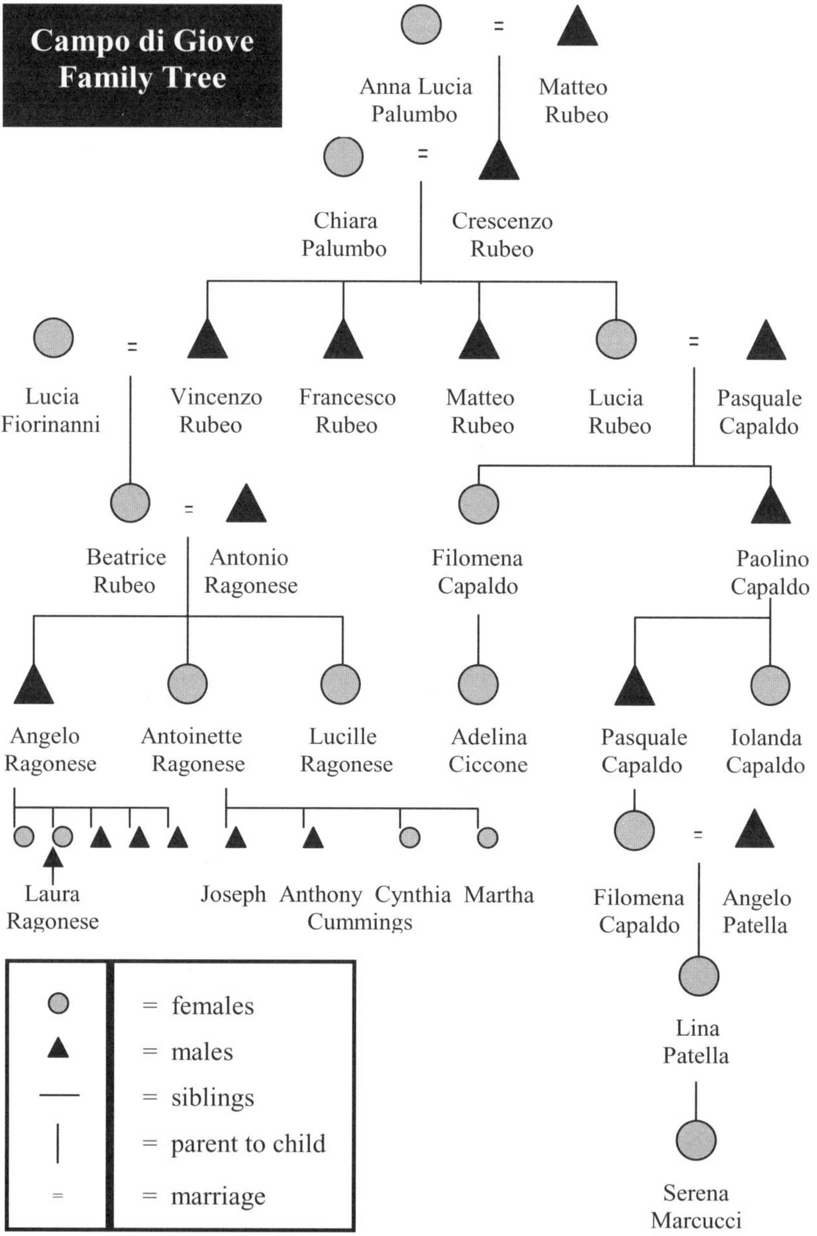
Campo di Giove
Family Tree
Anna Lucia Palumbo
Matteo Rubeo
Chiara Palumbo
Crescenzo Rubeo
Lucia Fiorinanni
Vincenzo Rubeo
Francesco Rubeo
Matteo Rubeo
Lucia Rubeo
Pasquale Capaldo
Beatrice Rubeo
Antonio Ragonese
Filomena Capaldo
Paolino Capaldo
Angelo Ragonese
Antoinette Ragonese
Lucille Ragonese
Adelina Ciccone
Pasquale Capaldo
Iolanda Capaldo
Laura Ragonese
Joseph
Anthony
Cynthia
Martha
Cummings
Filomena Capaldo
Angelo Patella
Lina Patella
Serena Marcucci
= females
= males
= siblings
= parent to child
= marriage

Chapter Five

WONDERS

Magliano dei Marsi, Abruzzo

The peace of the Italian dusk, followed by the darkness of the Italian night, were just what we needed as we drove away from *le nostre cugin*e – for each gave us a way to consider, in individual privacy, the images that had found their ways to our minds and souls over our twenty-four hours in Campo di Giove. We had a lot to mull over as we moved down from the peaks of Abruzzo to the vineyards of Tuscany.

Serena had been first in the procession of good-byes. She stepped back up on the curb of Via Supporto after she had hugged us and waved to us over and over. She promised she would study *inglese* in school and study it hard, so that when I came back to Campo di Giove, we could learn from each other.

Serena's hand had been holding the hand of her mother, Lina – who embraced us, and stayed in that embrace, with her thin but strong arms. Lina begged us to return whenever we could, and I felt the comfort that exists between those who have lived a similar number of years, forged a similar series of passages.

Filomena, the mother of Lina, had climbed down from the curb to squeeze us, as well. The gesture, from a woman who seemed more reserved, more careful than the rest, felt so intimate, so honest. She had moved well beyond her cold beginnings in the forest outside

Sulmona – well beyond the hatred that had inspired that enervating, nighttime trek through the mountains of Abruzzo.

Iolanda first hugged us from within range of her niece, great-niece, and great-great niece, but then crossed the street to accompany us to our Fiat. She needed to be sure we had her phone number and asked if we needed a snack. And she wondered if we would ever return to her birthplace and if we had enjoyed our visit to Campo di Giove.

Iolanda looked smaller-than-ever next to Laurie, and even next to me, when we bid our good-byes. She could not help but hide the look of sadness on her tinted cheeks. Her head was tilted to one side.

She did not want us to go.

I did not want to go.

I thought her sadness was about an excitement and a purpose we had brought to her life over the past day – that would fade when we drove off. I thought it was about reliving some of the stories of half-a-century ago and sharing the mementos of those times with people she knew would care and do their best to understand. I thought it was about the discovery of family, who shared as much blood as the cousins with whom she had lived her life in Italia, and I thought it was about the sadness of letting go of all of that – so soon after it had given her such joy.

But I didn't know any of that for certain.

I had to read the subtleties of her cheeks.

At the last moment, just before the starting of the car's engine signaled our descent into the surrounding valleys, Iolanda presented us with something that had been hidden behind her back. She moved it slowly around her side and held it up with both hands for us to see. It was a bag of *confetti* – not the paper variety we toss at weddings, but the kind that was invented in Italia, in Abruzzo, so close to where we were just then. *Confetti* – with sweet, colorfully-coated exteriors over chocolate and nut interiors.

"We use *confetti* here," Iolanda said, "when there is cause for celebration." She had tied it with a silky string and watched as we smiled and tried to quell another round of emotion as we placed the bag of sweets between us on the front seat.

"Please tell Pasquale and Adelina that we say good-bye," I said. "And please thank them for everything." Pasquale for uncovering the roots of our genealogy, for singing to us, and for bringing his ninety years to visit as he welcomed us to Campo di Giove. Adelina for showing us the *casa di Rubeo*, for inviting us to her 12th century castle afterward for *espresso* on her terrace, and for sharing the reasons for her black shoes, stockings, dress, and sweater. The death of her husband. The premature death of her son.

"And thank *you* for everything, Iolanda. We can't thank *you* enough."

"It was nothing."

"No, it was something. It was something very special."

Iolanda shuffled back across the street then – only letting go of the driver's door when we started to move. They were all lined up on the sidewalk. Serena. Lina. Filomena. Iolanda. Some with arms wrapped around each other. Others holding hands. Four generations of Rubeo women – gathered for our good-bye.

We waved and blew kisses. And they did the same.

I hoped Nonna knew as we passed by her family, her affectionate, generous, trusting, and loving family, that the letters of my childhood were back again.

CAMPO DI GIOVE
ABRUZZO

Dancing.

And singing.

Waving.

Kissing.

And real.

In Campo di Giove.

In Abruzzo.

And I hoped she knew that it was her Italian family who had brought them to life, and two of her American granddaughters, who still miss the softness of her cheeks, her ear lobes, and the safety of her hands, who still miss the innocence of the days when she was alive, and who know now, more than ever, as four generations of family slipped out of view and into the dusk of Italy, that she was magic.

That she performed magic.

And that she, quite obviously, still does.

....

The tears of our departure had to be silenced immediately as I battled the challenge of the curves and dizzying heights of Abruzzo at night. Out of sight were the aromatic pine trees, the roller-coaster images of the hills, and the fallow fields that were once sown, according to Adelina, centimeter-by-centimeter from there to Sulmona. "Every bit of land was tilled," she said. Instead, what was left were steep, curved lanes that gave no warning of their abrupt changes of heart, their fickle direction, and the urgency with which they wanted to escape the mountain chill.

A calm and peaceful quiet held steady in our car. It was a deep quiet. Laurie's hand was wrapped around the *confetti* on the front seat. On occasion, I could hear the crinkling of the plastic covering and could imagine Iolanda moving it from around her back.

The mountain routes led us into Sulmona where the wraps of nature had been replaced with bright lights, walkers, and dinner crowds. The city signs seemed out-of-place after our visit to Campo di Giove – where people and ancient manuscripts mark the spots of importance, not illuminated billboards and poorly-marked routes that disguise the path to the Florentine highway.

"Is this the road we came up?"

"I don't know. I can't tell."

The peace of solitude had been replaced with the fear of the night. The familiar Italy was nudged aside by a concealed one – where people seemed busy and clear about where they were headed. We were neither of those things, and the contrast was unsettling in the blackness that surrounded us.

"We should ask someone."

"Who?"

Our exchange with two couples in a nearby parking lot was brief. "We are lost. Will you point us in the direction of Florence?" Their response was simple. "Follow us. We know a shortcut, and we are going that way." And within seconds, with no contemplation of the danger of the prospects or the naïveté of our willingness, we found ourselves following that car, an Alfa Romeo, out of Sulmona and onto the back roads of Abruzzo.

The country roads outside of Sulmona, quieted by the absence of the city neon, were somber. We could not see into their car and were guided only by the red of their brakes and the white of their rear lights.

Their shortcut was windy and took us back into the mountains.

Their shortcut drew us into and through tiny villages and past cemeteries, abandoned buildings, and the limits of our personal serenity.

Their pace was slow.

The kind of slow that was either considerate or eerie.

After a number of minutes elapsed on those country roads, an unstated discomfort was introduced that made it seem proper, but impossible, to turn back – minutes that are written about in newspapers, in the columns where they address the spiraling down of human decency and the burgeoning of violence.

"Where are we, Lau'?"

"I don't know."

"What should we do?"

"I don't know."

"I don't either."

At home, I would have turned around or probably would have never asked. At home, I would have felt equipped to decipher the map, to know the streets signs, and to have some faith in my sense of direction.

But it was dark.

And I was in a foreign place.

And despite my familiarity, it was, and always will be, foreign.

Still, I was lulled by the culture and what it does to me. The consideration of "what ifs" seemed out-of-place there. Unwarranted. Unnecessary. And above all, uncharacteristic.

So we drove on and climbed up, up into the mountains alongside a well-appointed stone wall that guarded against the avalanche of a hairpin turn. I could barely make out the ivy that blew against the stone and the lights of yet another village that loomed a few meters away.

It was then that the vehicle in front of us slowed to a halt. The driver turned on the light inside his car, rolled down his window, and gestured for us to pull parallel.

So we did.

Slowly.

"*Signorine*, take this sharp right," he said, "and follow the curved road. Within a few minutes, you will see the sign for A-25. Just take it in the direction of Roma until you see signs for Terni."

"This road leads to the *autostrada*?"

"Yes. It doesn't look as if it will turn into anything, but trust me, it will. We were able to cut off much of the highway by coming this way."

"OK, then," I mustered with some doubt. "Thank you so much. We can't thank you enough."

"You're welcome. But it was nothing. We were going this way anyway. Oh, and my wife wants me to wish you a happy vacation in Italy."

"Yes, yes," as a chorus of *buon viaggio* rang out from the front and back seats. "*Buon viaggio, buon viaggio ragazze*!"

And so we pulled away – following their instructions upward.

Halfway through the hairpin turn, Laurie and I looked back to see if they would follow us or continue in the direction of the next village. What we saw was the Alfa Romeo reversing its direction and heading back down the route we had just climbed – and at a much faster pace than how we had just climbed it. Laurie and I inflated our chests, exhaled deeply, and smiled, as we allowed our faces to shine light on our disbelief and, at the same time, our complete belief.

Just a handful of minutes later, the signs for A-25 came into full view. Laurie asked me if I wanted some *confetti*. "In Italy," she said, "we eat them when there is cause for celebration."

....

The highway allowed us to catch only glimpses of the signs of the towns that dot its periphery. Pescina. Collarmele. Forca Caruso.

Paterno. Avezzano. We exited the *autostrada* just after Albafucens and headed north along back roads in the direction of Rieti and then Terni. Very Rural Route 578 led us farther and farther away from the lights and efficiency of the *autostrada* to the isolation of Abruzzo.

The largely abandoned towns felt more intimidating than quaint, more hopeless than the quintessential Abruzzo. Stop signs in the middle of nowhere made me uneasy. Smokestacks forced rivers of noxiousness up into the skies and inspired war-time images as the towers loomed against the backdrop of the moon.

So to calm the irrationality of the dark, I turned my thoughts to my *bisnonna*, Lucia Fiorinanni – the mother of the mother of my mother and the wife of the man whose sister's descendants we had met in Campo di Giove. The tiny 4'10" woman whose spirit, after the death of her husband in 1919, helped her to continue to raise and love six children in her new land. Thinking about her softened the human barrenness and the strangeness of the region's difference at night.

When Lucia's husband, Vincenzo, first arrived in the United States, six years before he sent for his wife and three children, he gravitated to a town in Massachusetts that had already been largely settled by Italians, *paesani* – those from the same country, or better, those from the same area in the same country, or best, those from the same tiny village. The Milford, Massachusetts quarry had drawn them there, to a lifestyle they knew and to a craft they had perfected over the centuries back home – in their carvings and artistry and manipulation of stone.

There were alcoves of Italy in Milford, alcoves of similarity and comfort – so much so that it was possible for an immigrant to enjoy the privileges of the new world while clinging to the amenities of the old one. Like language. As a result, years and years of my great-grandmother living in the United States led to her mastery of one English phrase.

"Cup o' tea?"

Apart from that, she relied on her husband and then her children and then her grandchildren to communicate the essentials. After her husband's death, two decades after they had been reunited in America, she opened up a store in the front living room of her residence on Cook Street – for income and for distraction.

"Her phone number was 1236R," my mother and Aunt Lu had told me one summer Sunday in the home of the latter – a home that remained just a minute or two from Cook Street. It was the kind of summer Sunday that was lazy, that allowed us to take off our shoes, loll around my aunt's round dining room table, sip tea, and step back into a time that was as lazy as that moment – back into a time when the two women into whose faces and memories I was staring loomed more youthful. A time when my older siblings, older cousins, and even I would prime the water pump from our grandparents' well and then marvel as the water made its way up into our grasp. A time when immigrants sold cupcakes and cookies out of their living rooms for pennies apiece to take one step closer to the dream they had been promised.

"We used to be able to pick up the phone and say '1236R' and be connected to her store."

"But how could she have run a business if the only English words she knew were 'Cup o' tea?,'" I asked.

"The store was filled with Italians," my mother said, "and we'd help her with those customers who didn't speak her language."

Our conversation meandered that day. I took notes but spent as much time looking up at those sisters, whose bloodline was marked not by a physical similarity but by a similarity of gestures, history, voice, and unconditional love for their family and for family, and of not having to explain the details of youth, because they were shared.

That day I learned that my great-grandmother's independent spirit had rubbed off on her daughter, my grandmother, and that society's limits were rarely embraced in the Ragonese home on Sumner Street. *Nonna* had worked inside and outside the house while her children were growing up in the 1920's and 1930's. She enjoyed crocheting and tatting and advertised her final creations in national magazines. She sold perfume, stripped and finished her own furniture, and worked at Solomon's Store in Milford center, where she sold yard goods. And she was first in line for employment when The Louis Fashion Shop opened at 187 Main Street, the very store that was responsible for my mother's going-away suit (a jacket with mother-of-pearl buttons topped with gold crowns and a predominantly-gray and pink-striped skirt with a waist whose circumference was well shy of my head's) in her 1948 marriage to my father.

"Mom would work a handful of hours each week. And when she wasn't working, she was on the go," my mother and aunt continued. "She took the bus to Jordan Marsh in Boston to buy us ski suits and reversible rain jackets. She signed us up for elocution lessons and dance lessons for two dollars a week. And when she wasn't thinking about us, she was out playing Bingo," they said smiling. "She was a fanatic – played about ten times a month."

I learned that she loved to write and had a great sense of humor, and often combined the two. She composed letters to my aunt in which she purposely left out all capitals and punctuation. "dear lucille it was so nice to see you last evening it was wonderful of you to make the trip from boston with *cannoli* from the north end..." Then the last page of the letter would have all the capitals and punctuation marks in order. "D L , I . I B N E. "

I learned about the driving lessons she took from my grandfather after he had received lessons from a Milfordian named Mr. Walter Mograss – in an era when it was frowned upon for women to get behind the wheel of a car. And I learned that she never got her license after she knocked down a mailbox and nearly drove the family car over a steep curb and into someone's living room. I speculated that her shoe with the clunky heel and the open-ended toe might have been partially responsible for her driving failure, and we all smiled as we remembered those shoes and the very things that they symbolized.

I was dreaming of all of that in the pitch of Abruzzo and was just beginning to replay the legend of Walter Mograss when Laurie spoke. Her words confirmed the discomfort I had been striving to repress.

"How are you doing?"

"Well, we're in the middle of nowhere and don't have a clue as to which way to go. Do we know what we're doing?"

"No, but let's just keep on going. We just might have to sleep in our car. Or just drive through the night. No big deal."

The light of our headlights was the only light to be seen in a swirl of 360 degrees. It allowed us to see far ahead and warn us, well in advance, of the nothingness that we would soon encounter. The nothingness. Until finally, finally, there was a fork in the road.

The fork represented a disproportionate degree of life – for at least we had a choice to make. But our choice would be random, as the fork offered little recommendation about the direction of Rieti or Terni, never mind Perugia or Firenze.

We shrugged our shoulders.

We ate some *confetti*.

And we took the fork to the left.

One hundred meters up on the right, out of the barrenness that looms on rural Earth, we saw the sign.

Hotel Residence
Ristorante
Magliano dei Marsi (AQ)

Yes, we are open, the gentleman said when I arrived at the front desk. Yes, we have heat. Yes, we are still serving dinner. Please, he said, let us help you with your bags. Here is your key – make yourself at home.

The likelihood that there would be a Hotel Residence at the end of the path we had traveled that night was infinitesimally small. It equaled the likelihood of finding a silver wedding band in the waves, of living a whole life without ever stumbling upon bigotry, or of watching a synchronization of falling stars spell out a word.

Possible.

But highly unlikely.

Within minutes we were seated in a multi-star restaurant and enveloped in windows that made us privy again to the splendors of Abruzzo under the comfort of light and shelter.

Besides the two of us, the restaurant had only one other inhabited table. The women there had hair that was as large as kegs of beer and as well-embalmed as corpses. Their hairdos, along with cockroaches, would rise proudly after a nuclear holocaust. Their fingers and necks were laden with gold and diamonds – both so heavily-decorated that I marveled at their ability to remain upright and to court food to their mouths without rupturing a disk.

In contrast, our hair was a dead substitute for a liver slab or road kill. Our jewels – an embarrassing relative of the rocks that lived comfortably on their limbs. What seemed a normal part of their daily existence would never, *ever*, wend its way into anything I would consider normal. Hair, I believe, should never augment height. Jewels, I know, should never elevate one's body weight by more than ten percent. Women, I trust, should never allow men to dominate an event – just by virtue of the fact that they are men.

But men dominated that scene. Their female companions were merely window-dressing to their puffed-up importance. On one side, an elderly gentleman with his back to us dictated the flow of energy and spotlight. When he spoke, often gruffly and in dialect, the others would turn their focus to him and respond accordingly – with a laugh, a nod, a furrowed brow. Their moves seemed more rehearsed than genuine – more strained than eased.

The other two men at the table were primping for their chance to take over his role one day. We could see it in the way they experimented with the elder gentleman's antics – mimicking his inflection, his body language, and his stature.

Laurie and I wondered if those two men were affiliated with the hotel in some way or were merely frequent guests. Their gestures and orders suggested the former, as wait staff scurried out of the kitchen to fulfill their requests – not as they would the requests of a common customer, but more as they would the requests of an unpredictable boss.

From a menu that was delivered to us in person, by voice, not on paper, by a young man with a dark complexion and rounded cheeks, Laurie chose a *frutti di mare*, and I chose a *pasta ai funghi* for dinner. I trusted that the mushrooms would be local fare – plucked from the surroundings that breathed fresh air into our lungs as we walked from our car to the hotel lobby.

As always, the main course was augmented with wine and bread. It was late; the *confetti* had done little to subdue our voracious appetites in our drive from Campo di Giove to Magliano dei Marsi. So the wine was more than half-emptied and the bread devoured in the time it took the waiter to interact politely with his more important customers before he walked back to the kitchen with our order in his head.

A vigilant call from one of the men at the other table, of light-skin and light-brown hair, who was dressed impeccably in a silk and tweed jacket, sharply-pressed slacks, and burnished leather shoes, brought the waiter back to his side and then to us – where our wine glasses were promptly filled, the wine bottle was promptly emptied, and another bottle was brought to our table and opened for breathing purposes.

"The gentleman would like to know if everything is to your satisfaction thus far," the waiter said as he bowed in our direction.

"Yes. Everything is to our satisfaction. Please tell the gentleman that everything is to our satisfaction."

We looked over, waved, smiled, and nodded.

Then we drank some more.

The food arrived in the amount of time that suggested it had been prepared with care, precision, and pride. Back home, we might have been perturbed by the timeframe. In Italy, the passage was marked only by the emptying of wine bottles, good conversation, and the consumption of bread.

As usual, the food proved *ottimo* – excellent. The mushrooms melted in my mouth, and the *pasta* was done to perfection. *Al dente* as it was meant to be – with a will, a texture – neither one of which was too intrusive.

My mouth was alive again, as it had been every moment since we had landed. It was growing accustomed to the visitation of dazzle, and it was happy to lay rest to the way it lives its life when it is not in Italy.

When it is dulled.

Weakened.

Anesthetized.

Disappointed.

Insulted.

And lying-in-wait.

But there, in Italy, it was alive. My taste buds were awakened to freshness and the presentation of grace. My nose was entertained by the aromas of the recent harvesting of the homegrown herbs. My eyes were blessed by the aesthetics of the presentation. My hands were happy to spend their minutes tearing bread to sop up the juices of heaven that slipped through the tines of my fork. And my ears were within shot of what I believe to be one of the most beautiful languages in the world – where words are delivered to honor a moment and not merely to fulfill a purpose.

The five senses live happily together, happily-ever-after, in Italy.

Laurie's and my conversation over dinner was always under the scrutiny of one of the gentlemen at the other table. We could feel his glimpse, his occasional stare. His involvement in our discussion seemed more inclined toward deciphering which language we were speaking than what we were saying.

We knew he would be over soon.

"I want to offer a toast to Nonna," I said, when the dinner plates had been cleared away. "It was she, after all, who made the past twenty-four hours possible, eh?" So we raised our glasses and held them there, as we brought her back to life once more.

"One day, Lau', a long, long time ago," I began when our glasses were returned to the table, "Nonna and I were sitting outside the old

Milford movie theatre in our big family car – the long, green car, an Impala maybe, with the enormously wide seats. My mother had to go do an errand, and Nonna and I waited for her to return. Nonna was in the front seat, and I was in the back. Dwarfed by the extra space.

"I had a little writing tablet, and on it I was printing several numbers, four or five digits long, for Nonna to add up in her head. Like 4,382 + 5,201 + 16,998 + 8,884 + 29,767. She was just sitting in the front seat – watching the children play in the park to her right and waiting for me to read out the numbers when I had finished writing them. When I did read them, she listened casually, quietly.

"At the *precise* moment that I stopped reading the last number, the exact moment that the last syllable passed through my lips, she turned her head away from the children in the park and said softly, with a near-perfect English accent, 'Why that's 65,232, dear.'

"From the backseat, I wrote down her answer and took a minute to confirm her total. When I discovered she was right, I squealed with delight and immeasurable admiration. 'How do you *do* that, Nonna?' 'How? I don't know,' she said. 'But if you practice, my *Martuccia*, (Martoocha) if you practice, I know you will be able to, too. Now, in the meantime, why don't you give me another, and I will see if I can figure out how to explain it to you.'"

I smiled then, back in Abruzzo, as I remembered the moment and the sound of my *nonna's* voice when she called me her *Martuccia* – a diminutive for Martha. Marta.

I smiled the kind of smile that makes a noise.

And found myself staring straight ahead.

Into nothingness.

And there I dawdled, until I was in that backseat again, on the Main Street of Milford, across from the old movie theatre, in our old family car. At a time when my black hair was cut with a bowl and my PF Flyers were used as brakes for my purple banana seat bicycle. When I would flex my bony biceps and talk with a lisp and race home at 5:30 PM to watch *Superman* on Channel 56. When I could climb onto my brother Joseph's back and take off down the icy streets on a Flexible Flyer. When I would sit up on a grandparent's lap and tuck my head into the space between her head and her shoulder and wonder if the magic of her tooth trick and her math genius would ever rub off on me.

When I spoke again, I had tears in my eyes.

"So here's to Nonna," I finally said. And we clinked our glasses and let the red wine splash against our tongues and the roofs of our mouths and our teeth and let it slip down our throats.

"...You know, if I could have a handful of wishes, Laurie, I would wish Nonna were sitting right at this table with us. Right here. Right now. I'd rattle off a string of numbers and watch as she solved them with ease. I would then get up from my chair, place my two hands on her soft cheeks, and say, 'How can you do that, Nonna?' And then I would kiss her face. First one side. And then the other side. And then the other side. And then the other. Again and again."

"If *I* could have a handful of wishes," Laurie said with tears in *her* eyes, "a handful of wishes, I would wish my father had come here just once before he died. I would wish he could have seen what we saw today. I would wish he could have met the relatives and seen this beauty and eaten this food and celebrated his roots. He would have *loved* it here. I *know* it. I *know* it."

When she finished speaking, we clinked glasses once more and emptied them, and by the time we had wiped our cheeks and cooled our stinging eyes and exhaled deeply, complimentary *grappa* was being brought to our table, and the gentleman who had been spying on our words and our sensibilities rose from his chair and made his way to our sides.

....

Grappa, someone once told me, is made from the vines of grapes. But it packs much more of a punch than would be expected from processed sticks.

Grappa has the potency and the sting of kerosene. It sears the flesh off of the esophageal corridors, annihilates the remnants of flavor on an after-dinner tongue, and summons a fiery hell from the bilious digestive tract. Because of all of that, and much more, *grappa* and I will forever remain acquaintances. It is a flavor or an experience for which I would never gain an appreciation or acquire a taste.

Its arrival at our table in Abruzzo, therefore, was met with restrained disappointment. I would have preferred *Vino Santo con biscotti* to a flammable, liquid stick – the kind of stick that could be caressed to ignite a flame on a Girl Scout camping trip. But its consumption in Abruzzo was required, born out of a need to feel more polite than honest.

"Do you like *grappa*?" he asked when he pulled out a chair.

"Oh, yes, we *love grappa*."

"So, you've had it before."

"Yes, we've had it before."

"*Bravissime.* So, what brings you two to Magliano dei Marsi?"

"Luck."

"What do you mean?" he asked as he nodded his head, beckoning me to fill in the blanks. At the same time, he grabbed hold of the wooden seat and pulled his chair closer to the table.

Laurie waited as I provided the reasons for our trip to Italy and how we had spent the past two days. She had heard it enough now that she could follow the progression in *italiano*, could mention at exactly the right time that I should say this or remark on that.

He was interested. I could tell by the way his eyes stared into mine, uninterrupted – by the way his mouth was held slightly agape. He was filled with a proud awe and was intrigued that we felt compelled to journey back to Abruzzo, his region, to uncover what was clearly dear to us.

"Are you both Italian?" he asked during a rare interruption.

"Half. Laura is Italian and German."

"Her last name?"

"Ragonese. Rah♪Go♫Nay♪Zay♪."

"That's a Sicilian name."

"Yes. Our grandfather was born outside of Palermo."

"And you? Your name?"

"Marta."

"Marta Ragonese, eh?"

"No. No. Marta Cummings."

If I had taken a small revolver and pointed it directly at his temple or filled a test tube with hydrochloric acid and sprayed it into his eyes just then, I would not have seen such a reaction to the truth of my last name.

"Coomings?" he asked, with his cheeks disgusted and eyes squinted. "Coomings? Did you say Coomings?"

"Yes. Coomings."

"But, but…"

"My father is Irish. That's all. My father is Irish. I am half-Irish and half-Italian. So, my last name is Irish."

"But you don't look a thing Irish. And she doesn't look a thing Italian."

"She has the name. I have the face."

He pushed his chair back then and left the table. We were not sure if the gesture was one of disgust or intrigue – an intrigue that needed to be shared with his friends.

His reasons for leaving did not matter to us.

What mattered was that in the wake of his departure, we took the *grappa* and cast it into our half-filled water glasses, causing it to swirl about in bold disdain of its plainer cohort. So bold was its arrogance, its separation, in fact, that we lived in fear that *quell'uomo* would return to our table to see the class struggle that was unfolding in our water glasses. So we swigged the *grappa-acqua* combination until the tumblers were emptied and our heads and stomachs were filled with bubbly water, red wine, and diesel.

When he returned, he returned for flirting.

When he returned, he returned with more *grappa*.

We wondered if reciprocal-flirting would win us dinner and if *grappa*-swigging would win us death.

Thirty minutes later, we were alone in our beds trying to kill the effects of the alcohol and wondering if our rejection of his offer to adjust the heat in our room would mean that dinner would *not* be on the house. Shortly thereafter, with the radiators just starting to kick in, we were singing the refrain that had been invented and mastered at our grandmother's wake – after each of the nine grandchildren was asked, over and over again, if we were Ange's (short for Angelo Vincent) child or Netta's (short for Antoinette) child and then asked where each of us fell in the age hierarchy. To eradicate the boredom of the repetition and to streamline the responses, the nine of us lined up in a room that was hidden from Nonna's closed eyes and covered teeth. From eldest to youngest we arranged ourselves and then crafted and practiced a rapid-fire-domino-ditty that was performed on first hint of inquiry.

"Now are you Netta's child or Ange's child?"

"Well, let us answer that for you. Places everyone. Ready?"

"We are…

"*♪Ange♪Netta♪Netta♪Ange♪Netta♪Ange♪Ange♪Netta♪Ange.*"

"Pardon?"

"*♪Ange♪Netta♪Netta♪Ange♪Netta♪Ange♪Ange♪Netta♪Ange.*"

"Oh," the person would say – caught between a smile, even laughter, and the absurdity of such a performance in a funeral home. "Well, thank you," he or she would continue before turning around and heading off to a more distant place.

"You bet," we would say, smiling.

It wasn't long before no one else asked us our hereditary link.

Back then, we did not know why.

Back in Abruzzo, thirty minutes after our umpteenth round of ♪Ange-Netta-Netta♪, the *grappa* was quieted enough, and we were quieted enough, to fall off to sleep. But the effects of the kerosene persisted for several hours, for I awoke to the hysteria of Laurie in her nearby bed – incoherent in her translation of the dream that had escorted her to the waking hours. A dream that featured her mixing a Martini (shaken not stirred) which turned into a Manhattan when poured. And then featured her mixing another Martini (shaken not stirred) which turned into a Vodka Gimlet when poured. And then another Martini and another and another. Her recall of the dream was delivered with a brand of energy that snowballed into insanity.

"Lau', it's not that funny."

"I know. But I can't stop laughing."

"You're sick."

"I know."

"No more *grappa*."

I'm not sure she heard me above her cackle.

Chapter Six

BOUNDARIES

Firenze, Toscana

Tuscan Countryside

By midmorning, we were on our way, having discovered that dinner (unlike the alcohol) was not "on-the-house" when we paid the bill. Our rejection of his advances allowed us, instead, to sing thirty verses of ♪Ange-Netta-Netta♪ in comfort and to let the effects of the *grappa* wear off in solitary hilarity – but forced 100,000 extra *lire* onto our bill. We both knew we would not have traded one for the other, and at that point on the trip, we knew it without talking about it. But by shrugging our shoulders, embracing a few of the Italian facial contortions that accompany the word *bo*, and smiling.

The roads surrounding Magliano dei Marsi were far less intimidating in an illuminated morning than they had been in a pitch-black night. The fresh daylight air matched our expectations under the umbrellas of pine trees and Abruzzese peaks – both of which had loomed ominously in the shadows of the evening but then offered a brand of beauty we had come to expect in that region.

It is easy to fear the things we cannot see or do not know, but refreshing that a simple introduction can turn fear to appreciation. The next step, I thought, was to avoid the panic altogether.

The back roads led us away from Magliano dei Marsi in the direction of Rieti and then Terni and then Perugia, my old home, on our way to Firenze. We passed through towns we had never heard of and would probably never see again, though they etched themselves into our memories: tiny trellises with remnants of grapes and vines dangling, old men on old bikes, young people on motorcycles, nearly-empty towns with one store for bread and one other for fruit, vegetables, wine, milk, shoe polish, crackers, and *Nutella*, and one more for *espresso, cappuccino,* and *grappa*. There were rolling hills, tall, blue skies, and occupations that were rarely, if ever, seen at home.

One house raised pigeons. We could see the birds trapped in hand-made, bamboo cages that were hung from the edges of the rooftops. The cages swung lightly in the modest breezes but were sometimes propelled to frenzy by the flapping wings within.

The pigeons made the same cooing noises as their relatives in *Piazza San Marco* in Venezia, *La Città del Vaticano* in Roma, and *Santa Maria del Fiore* in Firenze, but they had a decidedly different experience. Those that were allowed to lay their droppings on some of this world's most exquisite architectural renderings and those that were trapped inside a small crate laying their trademark on some of this world's most exquisite natural offerings.

"Why does one raise pigeons?" we asked each other.

"Food?"

"To deliver messages?"

"Can pigeons deliver messages?"

"Competition?"

"Do pigeons compete?"

"I don't know."

"We don't know what we're talking about."

"No, we don't."

I was embarrassed by our intrigue – that the pigeon-trade seemed a bit strange to us just because it was different. As our car swept through the Italian countryside, the implications of it all waged battles inside my head as did the tangential insanity of my unspoken paths. Before long, another tangent took hold, and Walter Mograss was back in my head, visiting once more from the night before.

Mr. Mograss was the one who put my immigrant grandfather behind the wheel of his first American automobile to teach Nonno how to drive. He directed him through the streets of Milford. Down Sumner Street. Along Main Street. Over the railroad tracks. Through the Plains.

Via the morning streets of Milford they would twist – past Sacred Heart Church, where my parents would be married, past Cook Street, where my great-grandmother owned her store, and past what was once the Ideal Theatre – the movie house where a nickel payment gave the patron a ticket and a brand new dish, where the Ragonese Family went, *en masse*, to see *The Great Caruso* with Mario Lanza, and where weekly installments in movie serials would be shown to entice fanatics to make an every-seven-day film pilgrimage.

Through Milford they would travel, until Walter Mograss guided my grandfather back to my *nonno's* home on Sumner Street. And then Mr. Mograss would bid good-bye to my grandfather and turn his tall, lanky frame to begin his walk home.

"Mr. Mograss," my *nonno* would say, "would you like to come inside for a cup of coffee?"

"No, Mr. Ragonese. I don't think that would be right."

"Of course it would be right. Come inside. Mrs. Ragonese will make us a cup of coffee."

"Are you sure, Mr. Ragonese? Are you sure you want to do this? I don't want to make too much trouble for Mrs. Ragonese. I don't want to make trouble at all."

"Please. Please come with me."

So inside they would move, and Nonna would ask Mr. Mograss to take a seat at the dining room table. So he would go there with his soft hat in his hand, to sit and wait for his cup of coffee.

Mr. Mograss was unaccustomed to such gestures in early-1900's America – when people had to be white, and a particular *brand* of white, to be respected, to have their contributions acknowledged and valued. He was unaccustomed to this reversal of roles – this reversal of decency.

As I pictured Mr. Mograss, my grandmother, and my grandfather sipping coffee at the mahogany dining room table, under the twinkling chandelier and beside the busy wallpaper, I wondered what they would have thought about the pigeons – with whom they were sharing my mind's cyc right then. I wondered if the difference would have seemed strange to them or if the difference would just have seemed different and nothing more.

I knew I would have to consider that when things were clearer and brighter because then the morning that had begun brightly had matured gloomily. By the time our tires first spun over the tar of the Chiantigiana – the internationally-renowned and meticulous patch-work of vineyards, wealth, and stone farmhouses, the skies were gray, the sun was missing, and the normally effervescent grapes were stilled by the course of events.

Laurie would miss the curled greenery of the vineyards and the magical colors of the region's swirling hills, both of which are often immeasurably enhanced by the sun that looms 93,000,000 miles away but still manages to pronounce its powers on the knolls and crevices of the Chianti. Laurie would have to return to see the shining fruits.

And the dual nature of their strength and fragility, as they survive the elements and cling to the vines to grow, only to be clipped from their umbilical cords to rest in barrels whose contents, in time, bring festivity and altered states to our tables.

She would have to return. Return to see the grapes on the Chiantigiana.

As if any of us needed a reason.

....

Ribollita, translated as the *re-boiled* leftovers of previous meals, is a Tuscan culinary reincarnation with a name that leaves much to be desired. But as the lunch at a tourist restaurant on the Florentine fringes of the Chiantigiana made its way to our table in stages – first the wine and water, then the *ribollita* and fresh vegetables, and then the salad, our tongues were lost on what it *was* more than what it was *called*.

Our total submission to the flavors of the feast was an omen for our existence in Firenze – where our eyes, ears and noses, tongues and flesh, would be wined and dined in ways that would leave us rested, nurtured, and in awe. After our first two exhausting, uplifting, and inspirational days with *la famiglia* in Italia – revisiting the spirit of our *nonna* and sharing words and memories and histories with those she had left behind, we welcomed Florence as a transition between the emotion of the personal and the emotion of aesthetics. We were ready for some anonymity, some English, unabashed consumption of leather, Piero della Francesca, marble chess sets, a *cupola* climb, and David. And a taste of chocolate or strawberry or coffee or kiwi *gelato* whenever we felt inclined.

Florence afforded us a facelessness that Campo di Giove did not. In Abruzzo, we were relatives, foreigners, and fashion anomalies. In Firenze, we were a lot less of each, for the Florentine streets bulge with the world – the world of admirers and those who gawk.

Laurie and I fell into those categories with a magnetic allure. She was as drawn to the market at San Lorenzo (tee-shirts, sweatshirts, belts, backpacks, shoes, *Duomo* candles, leather coats) as I was to the veins in the statue of David's hands. She was as risky in her consumption of regional food (boar sauce) as I was cautious in my viewing of the skinless artistic and medical human sculptures in the Museo La Specola. She was as enamored of the mobile yet statue-like street artist in Piazza della Repubblica as I was of the Parmesan chunk that lived next to my bed. She was as respectful of the elderly monolith behind the desk in Hotel Porta Rossa as I was irritated by those who come to Italy and expect to find the United States. But we were similarly and unreservedly drawn up into the pizza-size, blue eyes of Nicola, our waiter in our first pizzeria, and the frenetic pace and atmosphere of Il Latini, the restaurant that masters the frenzy and the rarity of the Italian way.

"Was I just screaming at the top of my lungs about how to make *tiramisù*?" Laurie asked over the din in Il Latini, where people line up more than one hour in advance to press the flesh for a first seating. Where cured meats and cheese swing over tops of heads as waiters dance about in a mirage of service and connivance, where strangers sit next to strangers and inhale shared, homemade wine, crusty bread, and perfectly-dressed salad, and where, before anyone knows what has actually happened, patrons order more food than they would have ever ordered elsewhere and where the waiters who encourage this march toward gluttony memorize choices of meats, pastas, soups, vegetables, drinks, and desserts with the same intensity with which medical students memorize bones.

"Yes, you were just screaming at the top of your lungs about how to make *tiramisù*. You were standing with your wine glass in one hand and your wagging pointer finger extended on your other hand, and you were issuing an edict about the merits of *tiramisù*."

"But did you hear the way the woman at the end of the table was describing it? She had *no* idea. I had to set her straight."

"You are the *Dolce* Queen," I said laughing and smiling as I watched my cousin spurred on to defend what we feel proudest of in our histories: art, culture, innovation, spirits, wine, and apparently, at that moment, *tiramisù*. "You set her straight."

"I guess I did," she said emphatically before she halted, looked up from her plate, and asked, "Did I sound like an ass?"

"Yes, *cugina*. You sounded like an ass."

"Oh," she said, before she burst into laughter, imperceptibly halting before she segued into telling the couple beside us, the Midwestern dancer-wife and her much older husband, another fragment of our tale of uncovered roots – as if to say that although *tiramisù* is something special, that decrepit books, generous town hall employees, and new relatives were so much more so.

We ended our dinner with a round of *biscotti* and *Vino Santo*. The saucer overflowed with the hardened biscuits that waited to be softened by the after-dinner wine. In-between bites, the couple asked the kinds of questions that confirmed their interest and, I thought, their envy of our connection to this culture and the madness that unfolded around us that night.

When the last of the *biscotti* had been wrapped in a paper napkin and tucked in our backpacks, the aging *maitre d'* offered a blown kiss through the air. His smile punctuated the warmth of his soul and his appreciation of the tiniest of things in life as he remembered, with a bursting sense of humor, my mistakenly asking if they happened to serve any *porco* (pig) instead of *maiale* (pork) at *Il Latini*. His smile also remembered my attempts at Italian in a room that was filled with those who spoke only English or Japanese or German or impatience.

"Why do you speak Italian?" he asked, as I pushed my chair away from the long wooden table. I struggled to stand up while the button and zipper of my jeans pressed against the flesh that separated them from the evening's assemblage of food: *minestrone, bistecca, piselli, patate, pane, vino, insalata, biscotti,* and *Vino Santo*.

"My grandparents were born here, *Signore*. I am American. But sometimes, many times, always when I'm here, I am Italian, too."

"It has been a pleasure *Signorina*."

"A pleasure *Signore*."

"Come again."

"I will, you know, because I rubbed the nose of the wild boar."

"To guarantee your return."

"Yes, and now, *Signore*, I seek the nose of the wild *porco*."

He slapped his thigh, blew another kiss, and then cuffed the back of the nearest waiter's neck. "*Porco,*" he said, shuffling off toward the kitchen to prepare his staff for the second seating of frenzy. "*Porco,*" he snorted, with one more turn back to our table to show his smile and to lift his head upward to the ceiling. Then he disappeared, and Laurie and I left *Il Latini*, filled with the memory of a nighttime of freedom.

There is order in chaos, I thought, as we rambled through the cobblestone streets of the Renaissance. And there is chaos in order. And there is happiness where meat swings and cheese hovers, where *tiramisù* gets its rightful accolades, and Italian is spoken well. And where Italian is butchered, and pig is butchered, too.

And there is *splendor* in chaos, I thought. And I wondered when, again, I would have the kind of evening I had had that night, when cousins pointed and strangers listened and tongues danced. I wondered when, again, *my* renaissance would swing and hover and dance in ways that expose my soul and help me appreciate the tiniest and biggest things in life.

Like *tiramisù*.

And interested strangers.

And *maitre d's* who live.

The handful of days in Firenze passed at a pace that was too fast and too slow. At the end, we knew that the independence of our actions in Tuscany was to be traded upon our touchdown in Palermo – traded for family and a less tourist-oriented reason for being.

When the propeller-airplane landed in Sicily's capital city, we climbed out into a denser air and under a heavier sun. Without a word of direction or influence, we moved our fingers toward the tar and grabbed a tiny stone before we climbed onto the bus that would take us to our rental car.

The stone was a Sicilian stone and, for the first time, Laurie was standing on the same island that had surrounded our grandfather Antonio for the first several years of his life. Laurie's eyes were filled with a happiness and a sadness that like to visit together in Italy. The quiver in my voice confirmed that the second visit or third visit, even, did nothing to quell those opposing feelings.

Laurie and I squeezed our stones as we pulled away from Palermo, with Laurie now behind the wheel as we moved closer to the coast and the mountain of our *nonno's* youth. The tiny rocks rocked gently, occasionally digging into our palms or thighs, and reminded us quietly, but purposefully, of where we were and how we had come to be there, around 100 years after our *nonno* had touched the same kind of rock, with the same kind of emotion, but for the last time.

When our grandfather sang *La donna è mobile* to his wife, his son, and his two daughters, and strummed the mandolin he had mastered as a boy, I knew he could have never imagined that two of his granddaughters – the younger daughter of his eldest child and the younger daughter of his middle child – would be those mobile women.

In Sicilia.

In Tusa.

Chapter Seven

V I E W S

Pettineo, Sicilia

Sicilian Urn at Pettineo

The farmhouse alluded us on the first pass through town, mostly because we missed the big landmark – the village's only gasoline station. The hairpin turns lured us farther and farther away from our bed and breakfast and closer to the vast interior of Sicily. With each aimless kilometer, the dread grew thicker in our rental car – a Daewoo that navigated the relentless terrain with the power of an upright vacuum cleaner.

My search for the perfect Sicilian lodging had focused on words such as peace, quiet, only Italian spoken, and remote, but there was a limit, and the cow with the enormous head that stared at us incredulously as we passed was a symbol of that limit. As were the scrawny ponies, the wild dogs, and the lone farmer, 5'2" short, with seasoned overalls, a wooden rake, a cap that resembled a railway engineer's, and the labored movements that took him in our same, endless direction.

In spite of the thickness of the quiet and the unspoken fear, we pressed on into the desolation of the region's largest island. Our vacation had long ago tossed our schedules and watches and anxieties into the wind. They would have to wait to be picked up back home, where we punched clocks, walked too fast, and ate breakfast in our cars. But in Italy, Laurie and I were free, free to get lost in the wrinkled branches of the craggy vegetation and the yin and yang of the Tyrrhenian Sea's blues and greens.

We stretched our heads forward and to the sides and forward again in search of that infamous gas station – as if we were on the verge of spotting a sixteen terminal Mobil Mart or even a Gulf with two pumps or just an Esso station with enough gas fumes to get a couple of *ragazze* going.

Twenty-three kilometers beyond the village, we agreed on two things – first, we must have made a mistake, and second, if we hadn't made a mistake, and our bed and breakfast were still ahead, we had no intention of staying there. The cow was not surprised by our backward journey. He looked, instead, as if he wanted to roll his eyes and utter something about the illogical inclinations of foreigners.

The farmer was nowhere to be found among the olive groves that dot the landscape like coarse hair. He had quietly slipped off the main road to tend to his crops. Sicilians knew, more than most, the meaning of the words drought and aridity and improvisation. Perhaps he had headed onto the land to address all three.

Sixteen kilometers back toward our recent past, we found the gas station – a modest facility that would pass for abandoned in our Southwest ghost towns. There, in Sicily, it passed for a structure worth noting in a guidebook. We backed up fifty meters to find, on the opposite side of the road, unmarked pillars that introduced a steep dirt path. The five-speed Hoover grunted through the gate and down the shifting gravel. More hairpin turns, more hairpin turns, and evidence of water ruts that had nearly destroyed the passage.

Flood or drought.

Feast or famine.

On the last turn, the 200 year-old farmhouse unfolded before us. It was dressed in stone, green shutters, wrought-iron, and a host of olive trees and olive rakers that rounded out a scene of perfection. The colossal, clay pots that had once held homegrown olive oil now nurtured the kinds of flowers my father could name with precision and that I could describe only as delicate and vibrant. An earthen roof protected an outdoor clothesline, which happily took the place of a dryer. Bricked terraces surrounded the home, and rich green grasses cushioned the antique lawn furniture as the sounds of a dialect welcomed us to a place that was worth a thirty-nine kilometer detour. Or a forty-year wait.

The three or four rakers were wrapped in light-blue aprons, and some wore matching kerchiefs, while the ground was wrapped in green mesh to catch the loosened olives. Up, down, up, down went the implements until the olives dropped to the nets and were scooped up by the natives' nimble hands.

They were light-skinned Sicilians with dark hair, slight builds, and an acute sense of hierarchy. I could see it when they hesitated to interrupt their task to respond to our "*Buona sera*" and our request to find the owner of the house. Our polite and hushed wait nudged one worker to the windows of the farmhouse basement. He called out "*Signora*" with respect and a modest amount of trepidation. No answer. So he shifted his position to the door and called out again, sweetly, with his ear pressed up against the wood. Within a second or two, he nodded and then turned back to convey that the *signora* would be right with us. And then he returned to the proper order of things.

Laurie and I waited in front of the stone farmhouse with our hands crossed, hanging below our waists, as if to make ourselves as small as possible or as if to prepare for the arrival of someone who would immediately warrant our awe. A benevolent matriarch, perhaps. In her own time, Teresa appeared, gliding toward us, floating toward us, in a way that cannot be learned. She had light hair, a mixture of natural blond and royalty gray, that was all one length and rested above her narrow shoulders. A blue, velour v-neck top and white pants hung loosely over her tiny frame.

"*Benvenuti*," she sang as she reached out to welcome us to Sicily. Her soft, right hand met my right hand as my left covered hers completely. Like the flowers that clung to the stone crevices and cascaded from the clay pots, she was vibrant. But delicate.

In an instant, I recognized all the beauty of Italy, of Sicily, in Teresa – each peak of smoothness and valley of comfort. I knew that she, like her homeland, would nurture us and awaken us and urge our senses to stir. I knew she would hold us in her generous arms and smile, laugh reservedly, and speak from her heart in ways that would let us know that we should strive to swallow life whole – each moment, each precious moment.

Teresa touched Laurie in the same way. I could see it in her face and in her body and in how she received Teresa's welcome with an unspeakable level of appreciation and familiarity. Laurie had seen that look, those hanging clothes, those soft hands, and the contour of those cheeks.

We followed Teresa to the western edge of her home. The bricks carried her as we were swept up in her gentle wake. The Sicilian landscape that bordered the farm dropped off quickly to an endless vista of hills, olive trees, and a dried river. Above, an ivy trestle shaded us from the remnants of the October sun. Teresa's arms occasionally tussled the air to point out a ripening olive or *fichi d'india*, fruits that reflect an essence of Sicilia with their prickly exteriors and an essence of Sicilians with their sweet interiors.

When we turned to the right and then right again, we had arrived at our room. Teresa climbed the two steps and gestured for us to follow her in, past the linen drape that quieted the light that eked in through the glass door. Tiled floors. Beamed ceilings. Enormous beds with precious linens. Ceramic sinks. On the wall there was a switch that when pressed shed light on a large, clay, olive oil pot that was nestled beneath the floor and protected under a thick glass pane to allow for scrutiny. It was a reliquary tribute to the ancient work that inspired this farm, and it was a reminder to its visitors that common items should be swathed in positions of prominence.

Oh, I said to myself, I want to live here.

Moments later, Teresa pushed aside the linen drape and invited the views of Sicily back into the room. "*Questa sera, preparo pesce. Mangiamo alle otto. A proposito, da qui, dalla vostra stanza, potete vedere Tusa. Vedete la montagna*?" I will prepare fish tonight, she said. We eat at eight. By the way, from here, from your room, you can see Tusa. See the mountain? And then the linen drape kissed her backside good-bye as she returned to her solitude.

Tusa, she had said. The birthplace of our grandfather. The one place where he still lives, long, long after his death. Tusa. From our room. And Teresa. Delicate. Vibrant. Familiar.

An angel.

....

Laurie took advantage of the afternoon light by trying to capture the beauty on 35 mm film. I recognized her hopefulness but chose not to spoil her fantasy. She could not, would not, capture the beauty. Not on film. Not on canvas. Not in song – but only in the memories of what we felt during those afternoon hours and how the land smelled, how the leaves rustled, and how our fingers tingled as they massaged the ancient grasses. "I was going to photograph you talking to that old woman," my friend Stephan had said to me on a Christmas visit we once made to Arezzo, in the northern half of Italy. "I could see you two talking in the park, and I knew that it was something special. But I decided not to, Marta, because now you will have to *remember* what it was that made it so special. And how you *felt* because of it."

So while Laurie framed pictures and unknowingly took one step closer to that understanding, I unpacked immediately, as if I would be staying well beyond our three-day reservation. Candles were lighted, Florentine gifts were examined, guidebooks were stacked, and clothes were scrutinized for signs of wear. And then I took off my shoes and socks and stepped outside, down *le due scale* to the white chair that was facing Tusa at the edge of the stonewall.

Thc grass was prickly on my feet, feet that had already lost their summer laxity. They, too, were being awakened blade by blade, second by second. Laurie slipped back into the room to update her journal and to give me time to visit Tusa. Alone. I moved the white chair closer to the hallowed place as the time of living between daylight and nighttime settled over Tusa like a veil. I could fly there in two minutes, I thought, but the drive would take much longer. Back to the coast and then up, up, up to the ancient hill town that loomed between Palermo and Messina.

But I could fly there in two minutes.

I could.

Then a light went on in Tusa, so I slid down in my chair and rested my bare feet on the stone wall to watch the show. Then another light appeared. And another and another, as if to remind the world that Tusa was still there. Four lights. One for my brother, I thought. One for my other brother. One for my sister. One for me. I named them and was happy to have them with me to visit our grandfather, our *nonno*, again. All *four* of us now, shining brightly on his lap.

The greens and browns and blues of Sicily were rapidly being replaced with grays and whites. The olive trees and stilled rivers were hidden under the onset of night despite Tusa's attempt to shine on their permanence. Others had joined my siblings and me in clusters. I wondered if the darkened spots were signs of emptiness, abandonment, and a replacement of elders with the pull of what we call progress.

Just then a dog howled off in the distance and was quickly answered across the chasm of darkness – until there was a chorus. I was surprised by how long it had taken me to realize that in Sicilia, dogs across valleys replace car horns, television sets, and busy plans.

I was crying then.

And believing that the dogs come together every night to rejoice in the illumination of Tusa. And then they quiet down and find a warm spot on a bricked terrace or under an olive tree or on the banks of a sleeping river to wait for Tusa to return.

An early evening wine break was needed to mark our good luck and to toast the angels who had protected us along the way. As far as we could tell, there was one bar in town which was predictably close to the gas station.

The bar was the hub.

Our arrival there in the Daewoo marked a grand occasion. The four men who were gathered outside at the round, Formica table tried to be casual, but their efforts were more than transparent. We were tipped off by their halted conversation and darting eyes and then complete silence as we passed by their table. Our nods and smiles satisfied them for a split-second as we made our way to the inside of the bar which, when we entered, had one person behind the stainless steel counter.

The bartender's gestures suggested a sense of urgency and frenetic professionalism. "*Posso aiutarvi*?" he asked as he dried his forehead with the base of his apron. Some of the men from outside, including many we hadn't noticed, filtered inside to crowd up his tiny space. "Yes. Do you have any bottles of wine?" "*No, no...*," he said painfully slowly, and then, "*Si, si, si,*" shouting victoriously as he shuffled his way out from behind the counter. He had forgotten about the two bottles in the front case near the window – a case that housed Perugina Baci, Lavazza Caffè, some packaged pasta, and two bottles of dusty white wine. "*Mi dispiace, mi dispiace,*" he mumbled as he wiped the bottles clean, seemingly embarrassed by the simplicity of the whole scene. Of his whole life.

Little did he know.

We had him wrap us his choice.

We wanted to wrap up his smile and dignity, as well. Instead, we made our way to the front door through the relatively large crowd of men who were waiting to feel assured that we had been properly served. Some walked shoulder to shoulder with us to offer their two-cents about the wine and to nod their approval.

Laurie brought the bottle to the car and got behind the wheel while I headed for our second mission that evening – to make a connection with our cousin Angelo in Palermo, the relative I had met on my first visit to Sicily with my mother. The Sicilian dialect ran rampant around me as I reached for my phone card.

The phone card remains a badge of the enigmatic qualities of Italy. On one hand, it reflects a technological invention and luxury that had long preceded any such commodity in the United States. A simple slide of the thin, disposable plastic and a call could be made to anywhere in the world for minimal amounts. On the other hand, the telephone booth itself resembled a 1960's prop holdover, from the days of orange mini-skirts, orange shag carpeting, and giant orange flowers embroidered on bellbottom pants. And the push-button façade, which disguised its rotary secrets, single-handedly screamed a mantra of Italy. We may, at times, look modern on the outside, but we will strive never to shed history for the sake of convenience.

I was much more than self-conscious about performing in front of this group. I could not remember if I needed the zero in front of the city code. I could not understand my Palermitano cousin very well without seeing his lips. I could not speak the language in front of a host of people without being embarrassed by my errors. And with Laurie safely ensconced in our rental, I could not forget that I was the only woman around in front of this eclectic collection of men.

The first man at the table, nearing thirty in age, spoke too loudly, had a wandering eye, and slurred his speech in a way that was commensurate, I imagined, with how much he had been drinking. Next to him sat a balding cohort who relished his perpetually-tanned flesh. His cheeks sported two enormous dimples, and his arms remained folded over his chest while the town around him prepared for the evening's entertainment. The third player was a man in his fifties. Large. Gray-haired. He wore a white shirt, dark pants, and a leather belt that resembled the equator in its effort to contain his perimeter. Beside him was a fourth man, also in his fifties. The last two ruled the roost. They were the keepers of the conversation and happily and seriously regulated to what extent others could contribute and to what extent their thoughts would be affirmed.

The dialect clouded my sense of the direction of things, but the range of their musings probably stretched from the future of Italian soccer to the previous year's Sicilian snowstorm to the proper way to grill *calamari*. But it definitely stretched to include their theories about our presence in their little Sicilian village, and it definitely stretched to include a blow-by-blow narration of what I was doing, how I was doing it, and why it was taking me so damn long to make a damn phone call – for despite all of my efforts, the telephone call to Palermo would not go through.

I slid the card in slowly. I slid it in rapidly. I checked to make sure it had enough cash reserve. I dialed 091 as the prefix. I dialed 91 as the prefix. I dialed with the phone off the hook. I dialed with the phone on the hook. I swore. I looked at Laurie. I checked the number for accuracy and said each number out loud as I pressed the buttons. I put each item back in its original place, stared at the pictures on the telephone, and then slid the card in slowly and then rapidly, repeating the sequence of events in robotic fashion, as if doing so would profoundly alter my future. Finally, I interrupted the new silence at the table beside me.

"*Mi dispiace. Non parlo italiano bene, ma posso fare una domanda*?"

"*Si, si, Signora*!" they barked out in unison, each climbing over the next to tell me that I did, of course, speak Italian well, and that I could most certainly ask a question. The Italians were more than generous in their praise of foreigners' attempts to speak their language. "*Due biglietti*," I had requested on my first trip to Rome, at a time when my vocabulary tipped closer to profane than proper. "*Si*. Two bus tickets, *Signorina*. Ah, you speak Italian beautifully," the *Tabacchi* store owner said with a smile and an explosion of kisses from his fingertips. "Beautifully."

"What is the prefix for Palermo? Is it 091 or 91? Do I have to dial the 0? I heard that got changed – that I have to dial 0 now when I am in Italy, not just from outside."

"No!" the wandering eye grunted. "No 0. You don't need the 0."

"Yes, you do! It was changed. Months ago," the larger gentleman sharply interrupted.

"Well, it isn't working, is it? So that *can't* be the prefix for Palermo!" the eye responded. "Is it? Does anyone know? Eh, Gianni, what is the prefix for Palermo? Is it 091? You don't know? Marco! Do you know? Sebastiano? Paolo? Amedeo? Hold on," the tiny man said as he jumped out of his chair to ask the bartender – the keeper of decent wines, decent dignity, and Sicilian prefixes.

"*Zero, nove, uno*," he cried out when he returned. "*Zero, nove, uno. Ma piano, piano*." But I tried that, I thought to myself. "*Ma, piano, piano, Signora. Calma*." Slowly. Calmly, he said, as he moved to stop the drumming of my fingers – which had not yet been affected by the cultural transfusion. They remained grotesquely disrespectful to the pace of the rotary. The pace of Italy.

"Wait, wait," he cautioned again as he ran inside and then arrived back by my side carrying a cigarette lighter. "Here, now go ahead," he said, while he scared away the darkness from the metal buttons. "*Zero, nove, uno. Brava. Brava*." Within seconds, I was connected. And so were they, to every single syllable that sputtered between my lips.

"Yes, Angelo. It's Marta, your cousin. How are you? How is Angela? Oh, I am fine. Laura is fine. Yes, tomorrow. *Domani* would be great. First, we're going to Tusa, and then we will come to Palermo. We will call you when we get to the city. OK, cousin? OK, we will call you tomorrow at 4:00 PM from Palermo. Yes. And *then* we will arrange where to meet. Thank you, Angelo. Thank you. Until tomorrow. Until tomorrow at 4:00 PM."

I had been talking remarkably loudly.

And barely had time to replace the receiver when a united concert of "Where are you from?" resonated through the skies.

"I'm from the United States," I said, before apologizing for casting volume on their beautiful language in the interest of comprehension.

"Oh. America. So you are rich, then."

"Heh," I said as I threw my head back and smiled. "Not *all* of us have lots of money, you know."

"Right," they said laughing aloud as they elbowed each other's sides and waited to see what kind of reaction their gesture would inspire.

I started to walk to the car then.

"Wait, *Signora,* wait. Why *are* you here? In our little village? Here in Sicilia?"

"To spend all my American money," I said with a smile and a swirl of a hand that brought life to my gentle sarcasm.

"No, really, *Signora*. Why?"

"Well," I said slowly, quietly, "my grandfather was born here, in Sicily, more than 100 years ago. Right there, in fact, in Tusa," I murmured as my eyes, and then their eyes, met the lights of the hill town that would lure us tomorrow. "I like to come here as often as I can."

"So, then, *piccola*," one said, "we are proud to welcome you back." And then a leader of the table stood, and the others followed, all with somber faces and raised glasses, as the gentleman offered a simple toast. "*Alla storia. Alle radici. Alla famiglia.*"

The sounds of clinking glasses only quieted when they turned toward *me* to watch as I raised my arm to join them in tribute.

To history.

To roots.

To family.

To all that is real.

All that is lasting.

Chapter Eight

W H I S P E R S

Tusa, Sicilia

The farmhouse kitchen was empty by the time Laurie and I arrived in the morning. Just hours before, the heavy table in the center of the room had served as the site of an extraordinary multi-course dinner that Teresa had prepared with seemingly little effort and no angst – fish, yes, but also pasta with peppers, olives, and tomatoes; potatoes with sausages and greens; fava beans with fennel; cheese and potato casserole; pistachio ice cream; olives; and after-dinner drinks of Averna and homemade lemon liqueur. Memories of it inspire me and then deflate me, because recipes and ingredients and settings like that are so far away from where I live, where food is frozen, olive oil is not made in the basement of my home, and company does not take time to talk about the splendor of a grandmother's recipes.

The table that morning was quiet but filled with evidence of where we were. Fresh bread. *Parmigiano* and *Bel Paese* cheese. Several stove-top *espresso*-makers. Fresh fruit. Olives ripening more quickly in a jar of water. Tiny packages of melba toast. And a ceramic condiment container with *Zucchero* painted on the front.

Laurie and I assembled a breakfast we would never have at home, pushing aside our omelets, bagels, and cold cereals to make room for softened cheese on melba squares, a pear, an olive or two, a ripped section of fresh bread, and a snap of *espresso* to get us going.

We were headed to Tusa.

The birthplace of our *nonno*.

My mother told me that her father could play the guitar and the mandolin beautifully and that he would mimic the tones and the ranges of the best Italian singers after listening to them on his old Victrola. He especially loved the opera, and my mother remembers that he decorated their home with the sounds of *O sole mio*, *Santa Lucia*, and *La donna è mobile* – particularly on confirmations or holidays or graduations. And if they knew the song, his children would accompany him. Laurie's father on the violin, my mother on the piano, and our aunt in voice. They knew their father relished the moments when he could wrap his family in the world and the culture he had bid good-bye to as a young man.

It was for that reason that Laurie and I walked into a Florentine music store just prior to flying to Sicily to purchase *Viaggio italiano* by Andrea Bocelli. As we began the climb to Tusa, up, up the nine kilometer route, Laurie slipped it into the cassette deck, and we stopped speaking to each other.

Instead, I spoke to myself and imagined my *nonno's* long-lost guitar and mandolin on my wall or even in my own hands, where I could make my fingers become his fingers. Or where I could hear his voice, for the first time, with his Italian accent, singing us to sleep or encouraging us to dig up our roots and take pride in what his past, my past, had offered up to make this earth a richer place.

Within seconds, we were flying.

As if buoyed by the wings of our *nonno*.

We sailed up the winding paths from the water to the hill as Bocelli's voice engulfed the car and the olive groves and the vineyards with an indescribable emotion. Laurie and I cried and laughed and yelled aloud and knew that we were enjoying a complete return to little girlhood – when we could not wait to dance wildly in front of a mirror or make angels in the snow.

We dreamed, as we drove, of our arms scissoring up and down, trying to live in the moment and repress the reality that, before long, we would have to wait another endless year or even longer before our bodies could drop to the earth and be allowed to play and laugh and fly, fly like angels, with angels, to Tusa.

I looked over at Laurie. She was quiet still – maneuvering the ascent with skill and determination. I turned my face to the right to try to hide the tears that were then streaming down my cheeks in waves. I could no longer see through the window. Something happens to me here, I said to myself. Something that does not happen anywhere else, I whispered to the Sicilian morning.

When I did speak, I said half of what was in my head, and I silenced my wish, my need, to explain it all and to explain it well beyond my current understanding. What came out, instead, was simple. That this is where it all began for our grandfather. And that he never, ever returned.

"So we return for him," Laurie said. "This would have made him so happy. He'd be so proud of us. That we are here in Tusa. Back where he was born."

When she finished speaking, we both reached forward to turn up the volume, to entice *Panis angelicus* to sweep through the car and out onto the livelihood of Sicily. But just before our hands reached our destination, ever-so-slightly, ever-so-sweetly, the music in the car grew louder and then a bit louder and then louder still. So we moved our hands back to our laps and then to our lips, before our car skipped faster up the hill, to the place where our *nonno* still lives.

The first stop was the Tusan cemetery, located just down from the peak of the village with a view that rivals eternity: sloping hills, olive trees with tops that form the v-shapes of birds' wings, grapes, and the nearby Tyrrhenian Sea – with swirls of rich blue, bright green, and long, rectangular stretches of muddy tracks where the pull of the tide sweeps up the water's floor.

From this vantage point over the years, we could have watched scores of warriors stake their claims over Sicily – affecting language, architecture, and the appearance of the island's people. But then we saw only sunlight and peaceful ships, farmers pacing their crops, and cemetery workers clipping fierce vegetation, carving monuments, and watching us as we climbed out of our car.

We nodded back to them and smiled, too, but their smiles did not come quite as easily. We had to prove our sincerity inside their gates and convince them that our hi-tech windbreakers, modern camera equipment, and expensive American sneakers did not speak more of our obsession with the present than our interest in the past.

They would wait and see.

So Laurie and I stepped inside the wrought-iron gate – quietly, respectfully. We were in search of our great- or great-great-grandparents' tombs and any clues about their births, their deaths, their family story, and how they were presented to what they now know comes next.

We had already seen the burial extremes in our brief stay in Italy – anything from elaborate mausoleums with marble façades, Roman inscriptions, and oval pictures of the deceased, to open dirt graves under cemetery offices, where bones were mixed and scattered and almost laughed at.

Burials reflected their social tiers.

Way down deep in the basement of the earth or way up high, in polished stone homes, in altars close to heaven.

Emotion was thick in our throats as we tossed our backpacks over our shoulders and stepped along the first path. Our feet barely made a sound on the gravel that had been crushed to sand in various spots. Our stomachs felt nervous and filled despite harboring a modest breakfast. I could feel my heart beating in my chest.

We moved our heads side-to-side with caution as we read the host of Italian names – names that most Americans maimed but that flowed smoothly off of our tongues. They were familiar, because Sicilians had become Milfordians. There was the *cognome* of the town dentist, and over there were names from my mother's 1935 *Oak, Lily and Ivy* yearbook.

With the names came the black and white faces in those oval Italian photographs – photos that strove to bring personality and warmth to the coldness of the surroundings.

It wasn't long before we were guided to the spot. Two sets of short steps and one turn to the right under the morning sun brought us to the stone of our past. The stone of Vincenzo Ragonese – father of our grandfather.

"There it is," Laurie said, as I stepped up beside her.

"It has to be. Our grandfather's father."

"Rah♪Go♫Nay♪Zay♪."

The nervousness that had danced inside my stomach had, within a moment, forced its way up into my throat. I was conscious of my swallows and the exertion it took to repress first a hint of emotion and then a landslide of the same.

Our hands reached out to touch the oval photograph. We were the first two of our generation from "the other side" and the first of the generation before us and after us to see him. We studied his face and imagined his character. Upright, regal, serious, and proper, with royal moustache, contours, and tones that, despite being quite uncharacteristic of the Ragonese line, still carried our name.

Ragonese. Vincenzo Ragonese – owner of a *cognome* that is familiar in Sicily, where the name is nodded upon and embraced and sung. Rah♪Go♫Nay♪Zay♪. Names that live on are important in Sicily. Natives take pride in saying, "*Si, conosco quel nome.*" I know that name. Which makes us happy, as it offers proof that we never, ever left. Completely.

Vincenzo Ragonese.

"Read the inscription, *cugina,*" Laurie implored, as she edged closer to the stone to move her cheeks toward our great-grandfather's photograph. And then she rested her forehead in the hollow at her elbow's bend.

It was an inscription his own son had never seen.

"It talks of his character and gentility and loving nature. And it speaks of his children, his children, and how much they have loved him and missed him from afar."

"The children from afar?"

"That's our *nonno*. *Nonno* is that child from afar," I said. And just then my throat could no longer curb the anticipation becoming a reality, and I fell into the feelings – of death, of never having known those who came before, of separation and how painful that separation must have been, at a Naples port, where parents and child were forever parted. Where my *nonno*, in solitude, strove to balance his responsibilities with his emotion. Where his parents, from the shore, watched as their child left them forever, forever, in the ultimate act of selflessness.

Oh, what he had given up.

And what he had kept hidden inside of him.

Though I could only imagine,
as neither children nor grandchildren,
had had the foresight to ask.

Many years later, on a Tusan hillside, hours from that Napoli port and minutes from the family home, in a graveyard that remembered it all, the pain was alive in my cousin and me and ran wild on this table of marble. I was spent – from the relentless tears that emerged from years of waiting.

Our great-grandfather's face, *nostro bisnonno*, looked at us from within his oval frame and was touched, I was sure, by the years' failure to dim our passion.

I reached for my journal then to transcribe the tomb's tribute – turning to the page that held our family tree. I moved my shaking fingers up the branches. From me, to my mother, to my grandfather, and then to his parents' generation – where names had just become faces, and faces had become names.

My finger rested on my great-grandfather's position on the tree, next to my great-grandmother. There they were postured, forever, to look down upon what their union, their specific union, had created: an opera buff, an eye doctor, a quintessential mother, an anachronistic career woman.

Angelo Ragonese and Antonietta Macaione.

My eyes dawdled there, dreaming and imagining the young couple on the streets of Tusa, planning a lifetime together above their coastal heaven. A lifetime of children and laughter and music. Of working the soil, tasting the salted waters, and waltzing through the peaks of their culture.

There I rested, for muted seconds, staring, drifting, and sharing the fantasized moments of their youth, until finally I walked myself from the imagined to the real, from the ethereal to the clear.

"Oh, no," I uttered quietly at first, with my eyes and flesh still resting at the top of the tree.

"What?" Laurie asked from where she stood, wiping tears as she readied her camera for a snapshot of truth. When our eyes met, I spoke.

"I don't think, I don't think he's our great-grandfather, Lau'."

"What do you mean?"

"Well, first of all, our great-grandfather's name was Angelo, not Vincenzo. And second of all, our *nonno* and he were born too close to each other to be father and son. I know our great-grandfather didn't father a child at age five!"

A quiet was thick between us before Laurie spoke again.

"Then who is this?" she asked, having already traded in respectful tones for something far more casual.

We were well within view of each other's salty cheeks and puffy eyelids, then. Well within view of our complete submission to what we wanted to be true. I looked away to focus on his face again as I straddled the lines between weariness and imbecility. And then I spoke.

"Lau', I don't have *any* idea."

The slightest silence fell over us.

And then in the time it took a millisecond to pass through the calm, it arrived – having climbed up from within the bowels of Laurie's groin and traveled through her windpipes to the nostrils of her Ragonese nose – having wriggled its way to the surface to dance unencumbered. Undaunted. And free.

It was a snort.

A nostril-flapping snort. The kind that echoes. The kind whose independence leaves its owner awed or even scared.

Laurie threw her red face back and forth in unbridled hilarity, and before I could chain my impulse down, I followed her into the bovine world. Snorts filled the air – instantly transforming a place of sadness and death into a haven of frivolity.

Again and again to beat the band the snort arrived, never breaking to be stymied by this unfathomable sprint along the spectrum of emotion. From profundity to absurdity in record-breaking speed. Tears of laughter streamed unchecked down our cheeks as we prayed for a time when we could breathe again.

Breathe again.

Finally, my cousin trapped wind enough to speak.

"You know, I *knew* he didn't look a thing like us. The shape of his head. His cheeks. That mouth."

"What a couple of morons. Where're our angels now, *cugina*?"

"They're not here. I know that. They leave for a minute, and look what we do. Invent a relative and bust open like a couple of freaks."

"No one'll believe this."

"What're you kidding? *Everyone*'ll believe this! Everyone!"

....

In the hour following our paroxysm, we did a meticulous search of the cemetery. Stone-by-stone, mausoleum-by-mausoleum. Despite the earnestness, our desires did not alter the reality. None of the Ragoneses in our genealogical path had made that their final neighborhood.

The angels were still missing.

In the exhausted and thoughtful valleys in which we rested after our bouts with the emotional extremes, I wondered if Laurie were thinking what I was thinking – that the bones of our relatives could be nameless. Faceless. Without a marker to state, emphatically, that they were once inhabitants of this seaside place and ancestors of those who had led to us.

There are, after all, no oval, graveside photos of my great-grandfather and great-grandmother. There is no place to go to speak to them, to thank them, or to look for clues that shed more light on why I am who I am. Why I feel the way I do.

I fought the notion that they lived, now, beneath the ground in group graves. Not for what it would have suggested about class, but for what it would have suggested about how they were escorted to death. As if the quality of their burial would affect the quality of their afterlife. Or serve as a symbol of the value of their lives.

And their dignity.

On my first visit to Tusa, I had come with my mother to step upon her father's land and to find the home in which he had been raised.

On my second visit, nine years after that, I drove to the town's peak without directions, without maps, and without addresses. I had nothing to guide me except the memory of my mother and me outside her father's balcony – weeping, kneeling, feeling him so close again and so alive again. With only those memories inside of me, I closed the car door and looked up at the wedding cake architecture – piled higher and higher as Tusa stretched upward over the years. And sideward. I chose to climb. And then was pulled and wound and pulled some more up dozens of steps, past a church, and through a courtyard to a street that looked vaguely familiar. I walked the street, slowly, veiled, until I found myself in front of a home that resonated in much the same way – vaguely familiar.

Nine years of life had taken place between then and then. Nine years of profound and mundane had decorated and cluttered my brain. Births. Illnesses. Employment changes. Graduations. Moves. Reunions. But still, nine years later, some pocket had been reserved, preserved, for those things that are out of the ordinary. Such as a mother's and daughter's journey back to raw emotion. Back to family.

I stood in front of the house for a second or two before an elderly woman in her nineties poked her head out through the beads that swung in her daughter's storefront doorway. She was dressed in black. All black. I moved toward her to ask – to learn if someone knew if I had been lured to the right place.

A rawness clamped my throat again, as did an unequivocal respect for this woman's years and her commitment to this little Sicilian village. I asked permission to speak, and she cut through my accent with a seasoned and guarded gentility to grant me that.

"*Signora, vengo dagli Stati Uniti. Mio nonno è nato qui cento anni fa. Cerco la sua casa. Conosce questa casa, Signora*?"

"*Si, si. Questa è la casa della famiglia Nigrelli. Ma prima è stata la casa della famiglia Ragonese.*"

"*Ragonese*?"

"*Si, Ragonese.*"

Before I could thank her properly, I was crying. I now know that the tears that find their way to my cheeks when I am in Tusa do not flow just from my eyes. They flow from my knees and from my stomach, and they weaken me and draw up in me a depth of feeling that is more dormant back home.

In Italy, it is different.

The elderly woman took my hand and patted it and held it and asked me why I cried. "Are they tears of joy," she asked, "because you have found your way? Or are they tears of sadness," she asked, "because the journey is now over?"

Before I could answer, I paused to compare the *signora's* hand to mine – as each had been stilled in the comfort of the other's fingers, bridging the holes that mount between the old and the young. Hers worn. Experienced. Veined. Soft. Mine less worn. Less experienced. Less soft.

Life had gone on after my grandfather had boarded that ship.

But she still knew his name.

They must be tears of joy, I knew then.

Because the journey is not over.

The journey would never be over.

Laurie's first trip to Tusa was my third. I was happy to be there, again, with family. *Mia cugina.* She would understand the whys of our search and the tears of our search without one moment wasted on explanation.

Laurie parked the car at a Tusan stone wall that stands tall over the thicket below. Five elderly men held court at the bottom of the stone stairs that we would take up and under an arch, past the church, through a courtyard, to our grandfather's street. Our presence captivated the gentlemen. We could tell by the stares, the Italian stares – the kind that is more personal than our own, the kind that dawdles, until the exact shape and depth of their eyes and then souls are clear, riveting, and deeply, deeply sensual.

The eyes encouraged us to stop and share our story about why we were there. All heads nodded when we spoke the name, and each man took a turn offering a Rah♪Go♫Nay♪Zay♪ he knew – each straining to best the previous, each underscoring his discovery with a bob of the head and a circling of the fingers and, every now and then, a hand to our shoulders.

In due time, the name-dropping was replaced by an escalating reaction to where we had chosen to park our car. There was disagreement in the ranks about whether that space was a legitimate one and whether or not we would be towed away if we let it stay.

I chuckled.

And was amused.

I knew that those five men lived nearly every waking hour of every day on that exact spot at the base of those exact steps – steps that rested ten meters from the parking space that was up for debate. How could they not know whether that space was legitimate? Did their heads simply turn toward aesthetics and away from matters of necessity? Or were they using the controversy as an excuse to strike up a conversation, to satisfy their relentless curiosity and their interest in all things that involve themselves and, then, most of all, others?

The debate raged on until one man, 5'4" tall, led us to our car to circle it for clues as he rested his chin in his hand. After weighing all the options, he finally walked us up a hill to a makeshift lot where there was a space. At home, residents would have hesitated to park a tricycle there. In Italy, Laurie wedged our Daewoo into it with remarkable aplomb.

Driving was, apparently, genetic.

The men were happy with the resolution and then watched us climb the steps under the arch, all the while waving and planning on waiting for stories of how our discoveries unfolded.

In Campo di Giove we had learned that town hall operating hours were, at best, minimal. Open Tuesdays and Wednesdays Only If Tuesday Is An Odd-Numbered Day and Wednesday Is An Even-Numbered Day. If Tuesday Is An Even-Numbered Day and

Wednesday Is An Odd-Numbered Day, Then Open Fridays Between 10:30 AM and 12:30 PM. Except In December or If A Relative Has A Baby or If Italy Is In The World Cup or If We Are On Strike. In anticipation of the same, we made the Tusan town hall our first stop – particularly since the door to the *comune* was open.

Two young women were seated on the window sill of the first landing. They were positioned as if in the early stages of blocking a low-budget play – turned toward each other and feigning interest in a memorandum. One seemed scholarly and cautious; the other was high-spirited or, as my mother used to say, "she was a hot ticket." She looked like the kind of friend who could have been trouble in church or in school – especially during home economics class, where putting darts in dresses embarrassed me and where modeling our homemade clothes in front of the whole school made me want to curl up and die.

Our entrance was their cue to ask if we needed their help.

We did.

I explained that we were from the United States and that our *nonno* was born in Tusa, right on that street, as a matter of fact, and that we were interested in learning some more about his family. Names. Careers. Dates of births.

As tangents ensued, Laurie listened patiently to the explanation – done all in Italian. Her genetic inclinations and familiarity with a host of gestures filled in countless gaps. Still, there were periods when the exchanges were completely undecipherable to her. Through it all, though, she remained patient and ever-aware of the purity of the moment, the absolute adventure.

The two young women, now known to us as Anna (bookworm) and Santina (hot ticket), led us to the top of the stairs and into their boss's office. *Il capo* was a tiny, strong-looking woman with a perfect blonde coiffure. Her face was serious to a degree that an underlying softness was uncertain, and her desk was ordered and efficient – a place for pens, books, a calendar. Except for the spent cigarettes, there was no suggestion of silliness.

They filled her in, and she did little to disguise her disdain. An eye-roll here. An impatient flick of her ashes there. I had seen this pattern before in Italy, so I knew what to do. I waited until the right time, and then I spoke. In *italiano.*

"Good morning, *Signora*. My name is Marta Ragonese Cummings. We are sorry to disturb you, but my cousin Laura and I have come from the United States to do some research on our grandfather. As Anna and Santina told you, he was born here in Tusa. His name was Antonio Ragonese."

"Oh," she began, with visible relief, "you speak Italian, Marta."

"Yes, I do. Obviously not nearly as beautifully as you, *Signora.* So I thank you for your patience. But, yes, I do speak a little Italian. I studied at the *Università Italiana per Stranieri a Perugia* in Umbria quite a few years ago."

"*Brava,* Marta, *Bravissima.* Your *nonno* would be proud of you."

I barely had time to bask in the glory of her perfect remark when she continued. "*Allora*, Ragonese. Rah♪Go♫Nay♪Zay♪. *Si*, I know that name."

"You do?"

"Giuseppina. *Si,* I remember Giuseppina," she said, delivered with a smile and a hint of pride in her own memory. "She was a short woman. Round. She owned a small hotel here in Tusa."

"Exactly. Giuseppina was my grandfather's sister. And there was a brother Giuseppe who made and sold ice cream just down the street. Both were born after my *nonno* left for America. Can you imagine? My grandfather and his own brother and sister never met. Never."

"*Si, si, si,*" she offered immediately. "I remember Giuseppe. His nickname was Peppino. Giuseppina was called Giuseppa. Peppino, I think, had two children – a boy and a girl."

"Angelo and Maria."

"Maria is blonde, right?"

"*Si, Signora. Bravissima, Signora*! Maria *is* blonde."

"OK," she said with a steadily emerging softness, "how may I help you, Marta? Tell me. Tell me all. I am here. I am here for you."

With one sweep of her arm and a whirlwind of *italiano rapido*, Anna and Santina were cast into motion to trace what and who our angel-returned knew best – Giuseppina and Giuseppe Ragonese. They returned with a small book, the size of a woman's wallet, which they promptly handed over to Pina. Held horizontally, the pages were locked by a metal clasp on the left and arranged chronologically. They were worn, but meticulous, detailing birth dates, professions, names of children, and permanent departures from Tusa. We started with the elder of the two. Giuseppina. Born to Angelo Ragonese and Antonia Macaione – our great-grandfather and great-grandmother.

"Antonia, *Signora?*"

"*Si,* Antonia."

"But I thought her name was Antonietta."

"Antonietta is the diminutive of Antonia. It means little Antonia. Like Antonella."

"And Netta?"

"*Si,* Netta is another. How did you know?"

"That's my mother's name. Short for Antoinette."

Right next to Antonia's name, on the softened, yellowed sheets, was the date of birth in 1896 of Giuseppina, her near youngest, and the date of birth in 1902 of Giuseppe, her very youngest – born seven years and one year, respectively, *before* my grandfather had departed for the United States in 1903. Family folklore, family drama, in fact, had taught us that Giuseppina and Giuseppe had been born long *after* my *nonno* boarded that ship.

Forever we had lamented over the siblings our *nonno* never knew. But Pina confirmed the accuracy of the data. And so the list of separations grew longer. And the myth we had written to fill in for answers we had never secured was broken. Again.

Pina pushed up the sleeves of her cashmere sweater and lit another cigarette to unveil my great-grandparents' professions. Angelo ran and owned a café. Antonia was *una casalinga* – a housewife. Giuseppina had three children, Giuseppe two. One of the two was named Maria Antonia – whose middle name was now familiar. The other was named Angelo – after his grandfather, not a Vincenzo in a Tusan graveyard. Some moved to Messina. Others moved to Palermo. The house remains on Via Alesina. Laurie and I waited patiently for some glimpse into our grandfather's history – his exact time of birth, the witnesses to his arrival. But the booklet did not reach back far enough to include details about him.

"*No, no*," our angel said, as she snapped the book closed and shook her head. "Nothing."

And so she dispatched Anna and Santina again and demanded the services of a man who had wandered into her space to observe first-hand the requests and the interests *delle due americane*. So they scattered, and she took another puff and asked us what was going on in the United States because we were the fourth group of people in one month who had come from America to Tusa to trace roots.

"And you spent this kind of time with all of them?"

"No," she gently smirked. "They didn't speak Italian."

"Oh," I smiled.

The threesome returned with more books. Different in height and width and purpose but the same in their result. *Niente.* Our *nonno* had been born too long ago to have been noticed in their records. Pina's abrupt gestures signaled an end to her kindness. She grabbed her jacket, clapped her hands to get Anna and Santina moving, and snuffed out her last cigarette into an ashtray filled with what I hoped was her biggest vice.

Laurie and I turned to thank them for their help and to try to hide our disappointment. We had come so far, and after Campo di Giove we had grown spoiled. And expectant. It was then that Pina gestured for us to pick up our things – our backpacks and cameras and journals and pens – and follow her outside. Behind Anna and Santina. And in-between a host of town hall employees who had emerged from their cubicles to catch a glimpse of the day's excitement.

Up Via Alesina we walked – the narrow, cobblestone lane of our great-grandparents and our grandfather. The houses along the way, in varying stages of disrepair, still climbed upward and remained upright, despite the ravages of time. As we walked, we fell into step behind Pina. She explained our purposes – to stop at the home of our *nonno*, to point out the *gelateria* of his father and then his brother, and to enter the old town hall, where records went back to times that my grandfather once knew.

The *gelateria* came first – long-since closed but not to our imagination, where the smoothness of Italian treats and the wide array of colors in shiny containers surfaced with ease. Tusa offered an explanation for the ice cream worship that runs rampant in our family, where, as a child, I would anxiously await the 8:45 PM head-nod from my father to signal a trip to our local ice cream parlor before its 9:00 PM closing. But I also saw it in my mother, whose afternoon schedule often included grape nut on a sugar cone, and in Laurie, who saved room for *gelato* every single day of our trip, even if we had already marched through the *primo piatto, secondo piatto, insalata, pane, vino,* and more.

While we stood in front of my Great Uncle Giuseppe's *gelateria,* this was running through my head and mouth, as well as images of him behind his counter, with white cap and white apron, barely tall enough to see over the glassed display, scooping out his *cioccolato, stracciatella,* and *fragola* with pride. I knew my *nonno* would have been a regular visitor to that store, if he had ever returned to Tusa and gotten to know the brother I was dreaming about just then.

At that very moment, Pina urged us on. After all, what I was really staring at was a slender opening in a Tusan façade that was trapped by a padlocked aluminum guard. I was wedded to an image of times more honest than these.

We moved up Via Alesina, my heart speeding and feet slowing. They balance me on the Tusan summit and particularly in the shadows of my grandfather's home.

I know the house now.

I have wept under its arms more than once.

And stretched my head back, back, to breathe deeply.

And to look beyond the rooftops to the clouds.

To most people who have the occasion to stroll down Via Alesina, the dwelling is nothing extraordinary. Just an ancient row-house with a wrought-iron balcony, green double-doors at the base, a decaying edifice, and aged posters plastered on the walls – posters that detail the city's social events or announce the passing of a beloved citizen. Items that, in Sicily, are often quite the same.

Yes, to most people who have the occasion to stroll down Via Alesina, the house *is* nothing extraordinary. But I am not most people. I am a Rah♪Go♫Nay♪Zay♪. And the house of my *nonno* calls me by my name.

For the wrought-iron balcony has my grandfather upon it – as he whistles to his classmates to meet him in the nearby *piazza* to kick a ball around. The green doors enclose chickens they would slaughter for an evening's meal, and the decaying façade, that eroding shell of love and separation, whispers that the elderly are still there and should not be forgotten, because they stand, having weathered the years and the good-byes as they still look down at us from high.

I know the house now. And because of that, I cry.

Laurie's eyes clouded with water, too, but there was vision enough for her to find her way, to where she pressed her lips against the door and rested her head like a child's against the wood. She kissed our *nonno* again. She had climbed up, up onto his lap and kissed him and welcomed his long, grandfather arms around her heart once more.

I knew she had succumbed directly to the privileges of being one again, when she had sat with him like a princess for his last birthday. But in Tusa, more than she could have many years ago, she received his lap with the wisdom of someone who had lived a little and not with the gentle ignorance of someone who had barely lived at all.

In front of his flickering candles, she believed that a grandfather's lap was forever. But in their dimness, she had learned that nothing, ever again, would be all that simple.

All that free.

The best we could do was imagine the inside, since the house was locked and empty. The keys were in the hands of my grandfather's sister's offspring on the far eastern edge of Sicily, in Messina. It was almost better that way, for our minds were invited to draw more youthful images of high ceilings, cushioned beds, tiled floors, and a sun-filled kitchen.

Anna, Pina, and Santina stepped back to give us space – not merely because we needed it, but because they needed it, as well. They were moved by our devotion to their town, a town that to them, at times, seemed too small, too old, and too uneventful. But to us, Tusa was the center of everything. We had not realized that we were there to remind them that they were standing on something invaluable, something that we could never find in the United States.

When the moment was right, Anna stepped forward to document the times. Photographs of us, one of us, two of us, three or four of us, outside my *nonno's* home. Energy pulled us into the embrace of the building and held us there until we climbed down off that lap to say good-bye.

For now.

I turned to his home to kiss my *nonno* then, for it is only in Tusa that I am offered such a gift. In a moment, my hand met my lips there, in the shade of his front door, and then they separated, allowing me to pat his tender, aged cheek once more.

In time, my fingers slipped down his weathered flesh to reveal a simple message.

Handwritten.

In pencil.

The numbers whispered.

Otto. Quattordici.

Eight. Fourteen.

Façade of Nonno's Home

August 14th.

The day he drew his last breath.

My chest stood still then. Until I finally turned my head. In search of someone who might understand that my *nonno* was right there.

Right then.

In Tusa.

Tusa, Sicily.

Chapter Nine

TRUTH

Tusa, Sicilia

We followed Pina, without question, as she forged ahead onto the cool, marble floors of the old town hall. Their immaculateness hinted at a precision that was hopeful.

Pina led us up some stairs and down some stairs and up some stairs and down some stairs until we landed in the basement somehow. Large, open, gray, metal bookcases held dozens and dozens of booklets, each marked with the years of births, marriages, and deaths. From left to right they traveled back in time. Anna, Pina, and Santina stormed the shelves and one-by-one exposed the dates, sometimes brushing off a thin later of dust from the cover. Each time they shook their heads.

No.

No. No.

Every book was handled and examined for its relevance to us – each record of Tusa's history – until the farthest to the right still fell short of our grandfather's 1885 birth. Laurie and I looked at each other in defeat. Anna's and Santina's eyes mirrored ours in sadness and fallibility. We knew all along that it would have been hard to compete with the miracles of Campo di Giove – where hope turned to reality each time it crossed our minds.

But just then, Pina raised her four fingers to her thumb and shook the collection aggressively, in the most classic of all Italian gestures.

How disappointed she was in the rapidity with which we had relinquished our dreams.

"*Attenzione americane*! Do you see this other room?" she asked, before she placed her hand over her blonde hair and pushed sharply against the door. Once, twice, three times Pina threw her shoulder into the wood until it jerked open. Then she ducked beneath the four-foot jamb and climbed below saying, "I'll be right back. Stay right there."

The lowest level was moist and dark and cluttered with countless stacks of tall, broad books. I was certain that the recent American pilgrims to Tusa had never made it to this point. The cobwebs gave that away as did the musty smells of places never visited. We knew we could not expect Pina or anyone to have the patience and interest to comb through the piles of disorder in search of 1885. And Pina's return, just seconds later, with spider webs dangling from her face and hair, confirmed those fears.

Until she said…

"Here it is, *ragazze*. Book of Births – 1885. Right?" And then she winked and stepped right up beside me. "Marta, hold this." So, with Pina to my left and Laurie to my right, the 1885 Book of Births passed from her hands to my own.

We had not been allowed to touch the records of Campo di Giove. In Sicily, things were different. The rules and order of the mountains had been replaced with rules of the heart. The nearby African breezes had warmed people's senses of what is essential. Touching the details of those long-missed was considered essential in Sicily.

My right hand washed slowly over the front of the booklet – two feet tall and nearly just as wide as long. I took my time, visiting every corner. *Be here. Be here*, I remembered. *For these moments will too quickly pass. And you will long for them when you are far away.*

Finally, when I could wait no longer, I reached for the corner and lifted from right to left. The front rested on Pina's open palm while Laurie and I shared the back. We turned the pages slowly, carefully, knowing that how we cared for those dates would influence others' chances to do the same.

The months passed, day-by-day, respectfully and with unspoken suspense. Until we found the page.

"There. There it is. There *he* is."

Its appearance was delicate yet, as with *nonna*, it surprised us both. The fact that our dear relatives' names are etched so beautifully inside of treasures that are housed so far away is overwhelming.

As we carry on living inside the borders of an American lifestyle, there rests proof of our not-so-distant claim to other lands. There rests all the proof we need.

Ragonese Antonio

Just inches from our eyes and lips – the official declaration of our grandfather's arrival. My chin fell onto my chest, and my legs buckled ever-so-slightly. Then, at once, without a mere suggestion of the power that loomed beneath my flesh, I started to weep as openly and deeply as I ever have. They were tears of the soul – tears that flowed up from the center of me and then spilled down my cheeks in waves.

He died before I was born.
I was born after he died.
But as I live,
I touch the record of his birth.

Pina's arm found its way to my shoulders, and Anna and Santina stepped away to lean against the wall and take the kind of breath that I could hear. Pina then moved her hand from my back and grabbed my cheek and pinched it perfectly between her thumb and finger. And told me I should read.

I cleared my tears enough to view the details – written by hand and in a script that signaled a time when handwriting was an art. The Official of the State noted the specific points of each birth in-between the details that were common to all. It was in his hand that Laurie and I first read about our *nonno's* precious beginnings.

My lips moved over each syllable in my best Italian accent. Quietly. Just inside *my* head. Singing each note. Savoring each beat. There was never a time when I wanted to be more perfect. Never a time when I wanted to make anyone, someone, more proud.

> ...Avanti di me...Ufficiale dello Stato Civile del Comune di *Cusa*, è comparso *Ragonese Angelo,* di anni *trentanove, Capitore* domicialata in *Cusa,*... *il* quale mi ha dichiarato che alle ore *po* meridiane *nove* e minuti _ del di *diciotto* del *corrente* mese, nella casa posta in *Via Alesina* al numero _ da *Macaione Antonia sua moglie*... e nato un bambino di sesso *maschile* che *gli* mi presenta, e a cui d'*a* i*l* nom*e* di *Antonio*...

Laurie was wrapped in her own moment of appreciation and clarity, and I knew it was the kind of moment that had to remain a mystery to those who had not seen what we were seeing right then.

And *even* then, there was no knowing or understanding precisely why it had the effect it did.

When our eyes met, Laurie asked for a translation. I could barely move, barely speak, as the very last words of the passage resonated more than any I had ever heard. In time, though, I *did* speak, and my cousin leaned forward and turned her ear toward the pages.

"In front of me, Official of the Civil State of the Town of Tusa, appeared Ragonese Angelo, 39 years-old and head of the household in Tusa… he declared to me that at 9:00 PM on the 18th of the current month, in the home on Via Alesina… from Macaione Antonia his wife… was born a baby of the male sex that they present to me, and to whom is given the name…

Laurie sloped farther in the direction of the words and then slowly bent at her knees and brought them to the floor. At first her head had fallen toward her chest, but then, from her knelt position, she looked up and nodded.

"… in the home on Via Alesina… from Macaione Antonia his wife… was born a baby of the male sex that they present to me, and to whom is given the name Antonio…"

Then below his son's name, in a wave of curves and swirls, was the signature of our great-grandfather, our *bisnonno*, a *cafeteria* and *gelateria* owner in Tusa …

Ragonese Angelo

… bearing witness to the facts he had spoken above.

I traced the letters in the air and then felt myself reach down to touch him. For he had touched this page. And nearly 100 years after his son and he had forever parted, his youngest great-granddaughter and he were reuniting a bond that had seemed eternally broken.

Be here.

Be here.

Laurie's eyes were broad with the wonder of childhood – so broad that I could see my own reflection in her boldness.

We were awake, *mia cugina ed io.*

So awake.

In this room of birth.

In this room of life.

....

Minutes later, Pina appeared beside us with another book. The 1846 Book of Births. She had already opened the record to the birth page of our *bisnonno* – our great-grandfather.

"Are you interested?" she asked, as she dipped her head toward us, beckoning us politely, unobtrusively, for a response.

"Are we interested? *Si. Si.*"

Pina read the summary while we learned the date and time of our great-grandfather's birth. And the names of *his* parents, our *trisavolo* and *trisavola.* Ragonese Vicenzo and Perrone Santa – a *sartore* (tailor) and a *casalinga* (housewife). Vicenzo bore witness to the birth of his son Angelo, but not by signing his own name, for he could not write.

Just one generation later, the signature of Vicenzo's son, Angelo, on the birth certificate of his child, was artistic in its literacy. One generation after that, Angelo's son, Antonio, had so distinguished himself in the Sicilian schools before he left for the United States that his scholarship was held up as a model for those he left behind. One generation after that, Antonio's daughter, Antoinette, was winning the *Dante Alighieri Italian Award* at her local high school.

And one generation after that, two of Antoinette's children had published books – one on the Medici Family as patrons of the arts in Florence, Italy, and one on the family's Italian roots.

From a great-great-grandfather born in 1803 in the mountains of Sicily, whose hands worked sartorial magic on his clients' fabrics, to a great-great-grandchild in the early 21st century, whose hands invent words that imagine the magic of those skills.

I looked down at my olive-colored fingers as they scratched the details of our lives onto my journal pages. And nodded to myself, and smiled to myself, as that realization warmed my body and my soul.

An ocean may rest between us, I thought.

But someone had certainly, certainly, built that bridge.

By the late afternoon, the Mediterranean sun was shedding a softer brand of its wizardry on the fruits that define the country. Pina had already led us to the doorstep of a distant cousin; our hands had found our *nonno's* wooden baptismal font in the *Chiesa della Madre*; we had obliged the drugstore cowboys at the base of the steps by sharing the richness of our day; a handsome elder, with piercing blue eyes, had introduced us to his donkey – a pet and a companion of a lifetime, who lived in the basement of his home.

And we had made our good-byes to Anna, Pina, and Santina – the three women who had brought us face-to-face with our history and who were nearly as moved by the unveiling as we had been.

The waning hours of the milder sun and the eroding minutes of our stay lured us along Via Alesina one last time. We could feel the fatigue in our eyes as we began to move down the lane and could barely hear the whisper of the gentleman who emerged unannounced from the side.

"Follow me," he said, before skipping ahead. He had heard about the Americans' visit to Tusa, and he had something to share.

So generously, yet so clandestinely, he shuffled us off to a remote room in the old town hall, pulling us forward by the tender movement of his hand and a nod of his head and by our own intrigue in the secrecy of the moment. He closed a door behind us and knelt on the alcove's floor, reaching behind a row of books that rested on the bottom level. A seasoned "Tsst" was offered more than once as book after book fell short of his hope. And then he found one, *the* one, which he passed to me, as his pride spilled over the room.

"It's in five different languages," he said. "And it's all about the Greek and Roman monuments and ruins in Sicily. Right in Sicily. Right in Tusa. It is a gift. For you. Please. I would be honored if you took it from me."

From his knees, I took his hands into mine to thank him and then had him sign his name, *Rosario Ferrigno*. His lips formed the subtlest of smiles – parting only to offer another gift. A serenade.

So we stepped back and then forward and stared straight into his deep, blue, Sicilian *occhi*, and the tenor filled the space with a sound that confirmed our visit to heaven. Up, down, up, down, he guided himself to a rolling cadence that made me marvel at the breadth of talent in that land and the extent to which music influences how they see this world and live their lives and tell each other in voice how it all should be done.

I could see my grandfather.

I could hear my grandfather.

When we left Ferrigno, with the sights and sounds of the magic of our day continuing to visit us, Laurie and I meandered farther down

Via Alesina, letting our hands graze *nonno's* door again, and letting our eyes lift upward toward his wrought-iron balcony.

Once beyond the tiny *piazza* where our *nonno* had practiced *calcio* against the walls of the local *cafeteria*, two elderly women appeared before us from the left, down a sloping hill. Mother and daughter – whose heights totaled 9'6" and whose ages totaled 165. Slowly, slowly, they moved and stared, arm linked in arm, dressed all in black.

The younger woman's voice punctured the calm of our saunter.

"I don't know you," the daughter spoke out at the spot where the lane split – one toward Via Marta and the other toward a northern view of grapes and olives and waters. Without a hint of decorum or hesitation, she said, "I know *everyone* here, and I don't know you."

She looked at both of us and waited for a response, which I soon provided. I focused on her words and her whiskers as her animation and rapid-fire questions echoed off the stone façades and bounced from Laurie's face to mine and back again.

Laurie murmured to me to tell them that she didn't speak Italian, so that her silence would not be misread as rudeness. As soon as my translation, "*Lei non parla italiano…*," met the *signora's* ears, I was interrupted – interrupted by the pointer finger of the 4'10" Tusan as it worked its way up, up to within striking distant of my 5'9" cousin, storming over the American borders of personal space.

"Tell her this," she said, as she looked straight into Laurie's eyes. "Tell her it is very important that she learn Italian. It is very important that she speak Italian."

Laurie's eyes widened, and her cheeks reddened, as confirmation that she had understood each syllable of the decree. "Tell her I will. I will," Laurie begged from under the shadow of the aged finger. "I will."

"She must learn that it is important to remember. Otherwise, she will forget. Tell her. Tell her that."

And then she pulled her finger away and linked arms again with her mother, and disappeared into the narrow alleys of the Tusan summit, as Laurie watched them walk away.

Minutes later, I was perched over a Tusan stone wall, placing a memento of an ailing, no, dying, friend into an island sea shell, and tying it with the silky string of Iolanda's *confetti.* Then I nestled it in a tropical tree that rests at the end of my *nonno's* street – where I knew she would be protected and watched over for eternity.

Laurie was behind the wheel of our Daewoo, listening to Andrea Bocelli and remembering and mouthing the words from old, familiar songs. Her brow was modestly furrowed, as if in study, memorizing, memorizing – so as to never, ever forget.

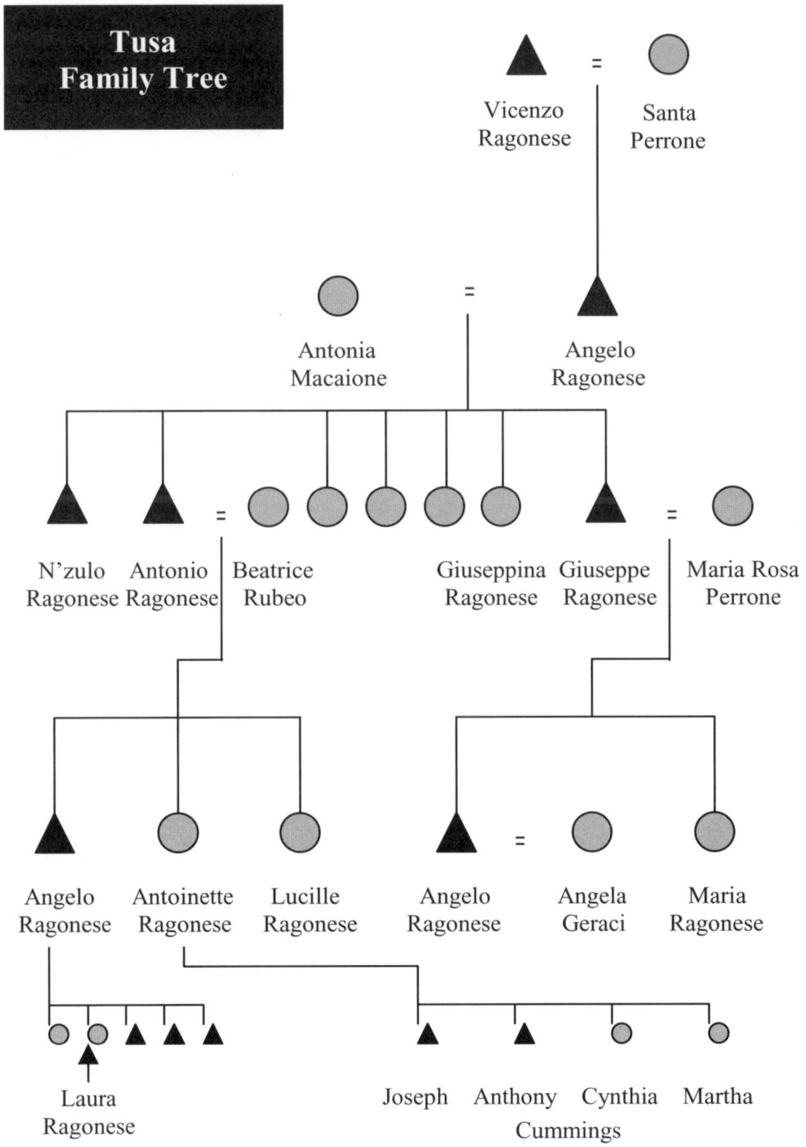
Tusa
Family Tree
Vicenzo Ragonese
Santa Perrone
Antonia Macaione
Angelo Ragonese
N'zulo Ragonese
Antonio Ragonese
Beatrice Rubeo
Giuseppina Ragonese
Giuseppe Ragonese
Maria Rosa Perrone
Angelo Ragonese
Antoinette Ragonese
Lucille Ragonese
Angelo Ragonese
Angela Geraci
Maria Ragonese
Laura Ragonese
Joseph
Anthony
Cynthia
Martha
Cummings

Chapter Ten

D E F E R E N C E

Palermo, Sicilia

The late-afternoon stop we made at a bar on the so-called Tusan outskirts may have brought the proprietors the single biggest cash visit in the history of the establishment. The request for "take-away" for *due cappuccini, due panini di focaccia*, a roll of cookies, two Oranginas, and bananas stymied the pale-cheeked, dark-haired young woman behind the counter and sent her into a multi-dimensional task mode that, according to the alarm that was etched in her forehead, was clearly new.

Several minutes later, we were on our way to Palermo – but only after passing through a stream of boys and men who had made innumerable treks inside the bar to scrutinize the source of the economic barrage.

We had barely begun our descent from Tusa al Montagna to Tusa al Mare when we tore open our picnic. The breakfast we had enjoyed in the 200 year-old farmhouse had sustained us throughout our day's adventure, but in the last minutes of our impassioned visit to Tusa, it waned in ways that had left us physically weakened.

The simple sandwiches replaced that weakness with another kind of emotion. The bread, square and crunchy, surrounded a *scamorza* cheese that had melted into the seams of the *pane*. The first bite was simultaneously exhilarating and depressing as the Ragonese blood in each of us chose to focus more on the sadness of depletion than on the joy of what still was.

"How sick is that?"

"Very sick."

"Do other families behave like this?"

"I hope so. I'd like some company."

By the time we found ourselves well into our westward direction, through another Sicilian cocoon between water and mountain, only crumbs were left on our laps and a melancholy memory of the best example in the history of the world that "less is more" in sandwich construction. What was also left was a satiation that assumed its happy place between "stahvin'" and "stuffed." But what was missing, profoundly missing, was the anticipation of our cousin Angelo's favorite method of underscoring his love for his American family.

Primo piatto.

Secondo piatto.

Insalata.

Dolce.

Pane.

Vino.

Acqua minerale.

And pressure to eat, pressure to eat, and guilt if one does not.

Our stomachs, therefore, were too filled for what was to come. We should not have eaten lunch. We should have had a sip of water and a nice carrot stick instead. We should not have eaten breakfast. We should have been satisfied to rub our noses against the melba toast and to dip our fingers into the homemade marmalade. We should not have eaten any meal the day before or the day before or the day before that. Why hadn't our lips been sealed shut, our stomachs stapled, and our bodies been allowed to shrink, shrink, shrink until each was a shadow of its plumped-up self?

Instead, we had made a profound miscalculation of time and quantity that would, in the late-night hours of a day that had focused on those who were dead more than those who were alive, lead *us* to feel more dead than alive, more gargantuan than we could have ever foreseen, and more entertained by the quality and quantity of a Sicilian cuisine than any guidebook could have possibly noted. Or warned.

"If Palermo came in a box," I said to Laurie as we moved toward the capital city, "it would be accompanied by a warning label."

DO NOT GO OUT AT NIGHT.
IF YOU HAVE TO GO OUT AT NIGHT,
WATCH YOUR JEWELRY.
WATCH YOUR CASH.
WATCH YOUR BACK.

And even though it does not literally come packaged that way, it is figuratively so – for terror is struck in much of the tourist body, turning those who could thrive in the island's capital *away* from its eclectic history and *toward* settings that are less spicy. We have bought into the ultimate big-city, Sicilian fear that the media espouse, and we have bought into a cultural assumption that remains narrow, both in Italia and all over the world.

Despite my disdain for those presumptions, I, too, felt the tension build inside of me as we moved from the sanctuary of the Sicilian villages to the pace and aura of Palermo. The streets widened into two-, three-, and four-lane highways as the number of cars grew exponentially with each kilometer. The tropical trees were outnumbered by humanity and horns, and an irrational shifting of lanes made me grateful for my familiarity with the twists and turns of an occasional video game obsession.

Faces that seemed affable one hour ago now seemed harried. Edgy. The metropolitan fear had its seatbelt tightening on me and was usurping every ounce of bucket-seat comfort as I battled whether the city faces were the same faces being viewed with different eyes or if the faces had actually changed.

"This Palermo map is huge, Laurie. I can't figure out a thing."

"Should we keep on going?"

"Sure. A little longer. I have no idea, though, if we are anywhere near Angelo's house."

"Why don't we go a little farther and call him from that gas station up there. He said he'd meet us, right?"

Angelo pulled up alongside our car within three minutes of my having settled down the receiver. He leaped out of the front seat of his giant Fiat and came around to welcome us to his hometown with a pride and genuineness that I found refreshing.

Angelo was a relatively short man, as were his father Giuseppe and my grandfather Antonio. Shortness ran rampant in Sicily. I learned this when I was privy to the carriers of the Madonna through the streets of Erice during a Sicilian summer a few years before. The whole of the United States would have been hard-pressed to assemble the collection of small adults that had been amassed, without a hint of effort, in that Sicilian haven.

The men from Erice, however, stood tall that day and night as they paraded the Madonna through the rolling, cobblestone streets to the beat of a John Philip Sousa march and a foggy drizzle – while younger residents combed their hair and talked on cell phones to friends who were well within shouting distance.

What Angelo was lacking in height, however, he made up for in other ways. He was a large man, solid, and used the full force of his arms to surround me and squeeze me before he took his right hand and grabbed my face, from under my chin and up onto both cheeks, so that his thumb was pressing into my right cheek and his fingers were making a dent in my left. Then he scrunched his thumb and fingers together, through my flesh, and tossed my head, front-to-back and side-to-side, before he surrounded me again with his arms and planted several loud, smooching kisses on both sides of my face.

I was five years-old again.

Laurie's welcome to Palermo was equally loving but diametrically opposed in terms of its strength. Angela, Angelo's wife, also small in stature, was just as small in the amount of figurative space she consumed. Her voice was tiny. Her role was clear. Angela and Laurie embraced gently and kissed from cheek-to-cheek. It fell short of the decibel levels Angelo and I mustered, but it did not lack any of the unrestricted happiness.

As they pulled away from their hug, Angela and Laurie did their best to explain who each other was as each grew acutely aware of the language abyss and how that fact, alone, would contribute in large part to the degree of their potential comfort and familiarity.

When we exchanged partners, I was able to explain who Laurie was and that her father, Angelo Ragonese, shared the same name as the cousin we were then facing, because both had been named after their father's father. It was Italy's custom, even in the United States.

Laurie told me that she smelled on Angelo the same cologne her father had worn. "Drakkar Noir?" she said to Angelo.

"*Si*," Angelo said.

"*Cugina*," Laurie asked, "please tell him that that was the same cologne my father wore." Angelo beamed with the translation, and Laurie did, too, having sniffed more of what it feels like to cross the barriers of culture with words.

....

Black and white photographs spilled out over the dining room table in their spotless Palermitano home – a home that still carried the gold nameplate of my grandfather's brother on the front door. The photographs were presented only after our tour of their meticulous space. Burnished floors. Zero clutter. It was a space that reflected a routine and an order that was refreshingly familiar. Refreshingly genetic.

Even the photographs seemed to spill with order. They had been boxed for years and placed in a drawer in a den in Palermo. One-by-one Angelo pulled them from the hiding place, held them in his hands, and either told us or asked us whose faces were there.

The photographs passed from Angelo to me to Laurie and then to Angela. Some prints of Angelo's father were new to us and made us aware that height, hairlines, and facial shapes had managed to travel across an ocean and connect brother-to-brother in ways that were not diluted by years, by distance, and by barely having met.

My grandfather died four years before I was born.

His brother died when I was nearly nineteen.

I regretted missing the opportunity to have met some of my grandfather some twenty-three years after his death. Of catching a glimpse of a voice, a mannerism, a spirit. A touch.

The black and white photographs with the wavy edges continued to spin around the table. Laurie's father, with taut skin and silky-thick hair, landed in front of her. My mother, with the narrowest of waists and a movie-star glow, landed in front of me. We are older now than they were then. Their youthful appearances had been replaced when we were not looking.

Antoinette, Nonna, Angelo, Lucille

"One day, your parents are young," my cousin Tom said to me in a phone conversation. "And then the next day, they are old. And you don't know *how* it happened, and you don't know what you were doing *when* it happened."

In the years following those photos, Laurie's father's hair had remained his signature, but his heart had not been nearly as resilient. My mother had more than doubled in age and liked to reminisce about her youth with a warmth that made me think they had grown up in a Golden Age. And that I had been born just a little too late to experience an America that was dancing to big bands, stumbling clumsily through an influx of immigrants with more honesty and patience than we do today, and holding onto the central focus of family – of grandparent visits and Sunday dinners with aunts and uncles and cousins.

"This was the eye doctor, eh?" Angelo asked, while pointing to the picture of Laurie's father.

"Yes, the other Angelo was an eye doctor," I said.

"First-generation American and an eye doctor."

"*Si*, his father was very proud of him."

"*We* were very proud of him."

"How did you get these photographs, Angelo?"

"They were sent from America directly to my father. He placed them in this box, carefully filing away each one, and he used to pull them out when we were young and talk about your grandfather and your family with a pride that would have made you happy." Then he smiled just before he said, "I feel privileged to continue to do my father's work." And then he grabbed my cheeks again with his thick, callused fingers.

They felt rough against my face.

And they felt smooth against my face.

And then he covered my right ear with his flat palm and said, "*Martuccia*, how about some dinner? Are you hungry? I hope you're hungry. There's a special *ristorante* I would like to take you to."

Martuccia.

Martuccia.

I stood and, from behind, I wrapped my arms around Angelo's neck and kissed him on top of his balding head. His cheeks blushed, and Angela beamed with affection in every direction.

"We are very happy to be here, Angelo, Angela."

"Not as happy as we are to have you," he said, while reaching for the hand of his wife.

"And, yes, I am hungry, *mio cugino*. What a question! I am, after all, a Rah♪Go♫Nay♪Zay♪."

....

Laurie and I spent the ride to Altavilla Milicia in the backseat of Angelo's Fiat. His gruff, dialectical Sicilian echoed through the car as Angela's more dainty, classic Italian helped bridge the gap between his language and my comprehension. My cloudiness was worsened by the darkness of the Sicilian night – which cast a shadow on an essential element of my ability to understand guttural Italian.

Lips.

Angela's Italian transcended lips. It was crisp and paced and mimicked a roller coaster – which helped pinpoint the emotion behind her remarks. The highs and the lows.

The Tyrrhenian Sea loomed to the north as we traveled east, back in the direction of Pettineo and Tusa. The sheets of light that covered the Palermitano skyline were replaced with dots of existence nestled in the Sicilian hills. A widening radius of black ink emanated from the points of light as we moved away from the capital and toward a more agrarian and less cosmopolitan pace and crowd.

The climb to the restaurant led us away from the waters but toward what lives under its surface. Angelo selected a seafood restaurant, famous in the region, and had come with his pockets loaded with generosity and a desire to toast us to the best his island offers.

Angelo and Angela were welcomed as celebrities when we entered the restaurant. They were regulars, appreciated regulars, and their photographs could have been mounted on the wall next to the other famous Italians and Italian-Americans who had eaten in that very place.

It didn't take my Italian cousin one beat to introduce us as his American cousins and to set the record straight regarding our connection to Sicily. I could picture my grandfather marveling at his still being remembered and discussed in Italia, by the son of his brother, some forty-five years after his own death.

"*Marta parla italiano bene,*" Angelo continued to the fair-skinned owner – also with pride. "*L'altra, Laura, non parla italiano.*"

I smiled at Angelo's compliment and was happy to hide the fraudulence of his remarks. At best, I was confused by about one-half of what he said, guessed at one-quarter of what he said, and was able to respond properly to the remaining fraction with a laugh, smile, frown, or clarification.

I surmised that his pride was less important than the symbolism of my attempts. To the Italians, there had to be only one *main* reason why an English speaker would strive to speak and understand their language. That reason, more than my skill, was the source of Angelo's pride.

The restaurant had the ambiance of a school cafeteria with its parallel rows of fluorescent lights. Simple rectangular tables were covered with white linen and white plates that had been grayed by dozens of forks and knives scraping across their surfaces. Straight-back chairs, some covered in a vinyl seating, squealed as we pushed them across the linoleum floors and up against our trough. Laurie and Angela sat on one side of the table, and Angelo and I sat on the other.

"*Marta – vino? Acqua?*"

"*Si, vino, acqua.*"

"Does Laura like wine?"

"Yes, Laura likes wine. We both will drink wine."

"Shall I get two bottles?"

"Well, maybe we should just start with one."

"*Due bottiglie, per favore*," Angelo said to the waiter, exchanging reserve for inebriation. "*E acqua minerale e pane*." Then, turning to me, "Do you like seafood? Does Laurie like seafood?"

"*Eh, il nostro sangue è Ragonese. C'è un cibo che non ci piace*?"

Angelo laughed out loud as he processed my declaration – that with Ragonese blood coursing inside of us, does he really think there's a food we don't like. And then he placed his hand on the back of my neck before ordering up an *antipasto frutti di mare* and singing its praises as the waiter wiggled away from the table.

The waiter's departure offered the first quiet moment since we had met up with Angelo and Angela at the gas station on Via della Siciliana. There were not any props to distract or entertain us – no introductions, no apartment tours, no photographs – just four members of the same family, three by blood and one by marriage, who, at the very same instant, had everything and nothing in common.

Silence was suddenly thick at our table.

Five seconds.

Eight seconds.

Ten seconds.

It was the kind of silence that strangers count and that would go unnoticed if I were with my sister.

Laurie's and my eyes met across that ravine of quiet, but we both resisted the inclination to break the silence with the words we knew best. Those lines of comfort would have been too exclusive for family. Instead, my brain's muscles flexed to find some sparks of conversation – which eventually surfaced to form a line of possibility, a backup for future silences: how long Angelo and Angela had been married, how they met, how Angelo's job was and when he would retire, if Angela worked, how Angelo's sister Maria and her son Antonio were, how often Angelo and Angela came to this restaurant and what their favorite dish was, how long it had been and how Angelo had been doing since the death of his mother, where his father's parents were buried...

Once the questions had been assembled, the next task was to pick those that were most readily translatable; but just as I was primed to serve the marriage questions, the *frutti di mare* arrived, and all eyes turned to focus on the eclectic array of seafood, some of which stared back at us through their antennae, softened shells, and beady eyes.

Nothing makes conversation unnecessary the way food does.

The enormous oval plate was placed in the center of the table, creating a reach that was equidistant for each of us. The Ragonese forks and spoons lifted from the table simultaneously while Angela's fork and spoon remained quiet and disciplined on the linen cloth. Scoops filled with critters swam their way to our plates in their basking juices. The juices were thin and lemony with hints of oil and spices, and they steamed up into our noses and eyes and jumpstarted our entrance to glory. In Italia, juices are intended to enhance flavor, not to smother the intricacies of the main dish.

Before the eating began, Angelo took his clean knife and pointed to each of the species on our plates. His fondness for the variety was not to be mistaken.

"Do you have *this* in the United States?"

"No, we have never seen this before."

"Really?" he asked, approvingly. "Do you have *this*?" pointing out another urchin.

Our plates were filled with *calamari*, swordfish, shrimp, crabs, clams, lobster, and a variety of unidentifiable beasts. And one-by-one, our stomachs were filled with the same – only augmented by the wine, the water, and the bread that we used to sop up the subtle juices. The napkin became our best link to civilized behavior as it rose repeatedly from our laps to wipe the corners of our mouths and to clear the remnants of Nirvana.

The Ragonese clan made three trips back to the oval plate. Laurie and I were knowingly packing a collection of seafood on top of the *cappuccino, panino, banana, cioccolato,* and drinks we had had on the outskirts of Tusa on our drive to Palermo only four hours before. In a marked contrast of will and restraint, Angela forked one of the *calamari*, savored it, and rested her utensil on the edge of her dish.

Wine glasses were filled again as the *antipasto* plates were cleared. Angelo made certain, three or four times, that we had liked, *loved*, the *frutti di mare* and then asked if we were ready for the next course.

Pasta.

Without waiting for a response, he called the waiter to his side, who was accompanied by the owner, and told them that we *loved* the *antipasto* and would like to repeat the *frutti di mare* in the form of a *pasta.*

"*Va bene*?" Angelo asked as he clasped his hand over mine.

"Yes, that would be wonderful," I said, before I began the translation to Laurie. When I finished, she pushed her seat back from the table to a barely perceptible degree, puffed up her cheeks, and blew out a tiny bit of air from the hole her lips had formed. "Great," Laurie said. "That sounds great."

In the aftermath of the first course, another silence followed the waiter's and owner's exits from our table. I was prepared, though, and headed full force into the questions I had on reserve. Both beamed with the marriage inquiries, pulled their chairs closer to the table, and grinned to a degree that suggested they were still very,

very much in love and that each offered each other something that no one else could.

They described their wedding day with the kind of detail and bliss that suggested it had just happened the evening before. Angela blushed, and Angelo pumped out his chest in acknowledgement that his wife's happiness could only be the result of his being an unparalleled husband, gentleman, and provider. He was horrified when I asked Angela if she worked. "No," he answered emphatically as she shook her head back and forth. "She does not work. She doesn't need to."

In deference to our setting, I nodded and smiled at Angela. In return, her smile was cryptic – as if she would have had more to say and would have said it if there had been room for that in their general and specific culture.

Everything and nothing in common.

That tangent of consideration was swiftly swept away when the *pasta frutti di mare* arrived. At least two kilograms (4.4 pounds) of thickened *spaghetti* were curled up on a family-style dish and dowsed with all of the players of the course before.

The owner took it upon himself to hoist up the *pasta* with two large spoons. He moved to serve Angelo first, but Angelo pointed to his wife's plate and then Laura's and then mine before the second phase of dinner settled before him. The aromas and heat wasted little time rising to our senses. My glasses steamed me to blindness before I removed them to focus on the *spaghetti al dente* that lay still on my plate.

When I took the first bite, my stomach, my buttons, my belt, sent me a clear message of fulfillment. Completion. Laurie started to escort her tiny shrimp to the side of her plate – both to avoid an allergic reaction and, I felt certain, to diminish the quantity of food for which she would be responsible. Angelo twirled his *pasta* and stabbed the sea creatures with abandon. Angela sipped her water and watched us embark on our futile attempts to keep pace with her husband as she started to make a dent in her portion, whose size was eclipsed by ours.

Midway through our second course, I turned to Angelo and mentioned that I was getting filled. My hand rested on my paunch, and I followed the lead of my American cousin as I inflated my cheeks and blew out air into the skies. Angelo dismissed my condition with a "Pfft," gave me a tap on the back of my head, and told me I had to do better than that. Laurie intuited the exchange and chose to refrain from speaking. Instead, I watched as her hand slipped under the table to unbutton and partially unzip the jeans that had once hovered closer to baggy than taut but that then hovered closer to *kielbasa* skin than anyone would have ever wanted to admit.

And so we plodded on, and as each of us had been accustomed to since our entry into this family, we cleaned our plates and even took the time to soak up the traces of juice with yet another piece of bread.

Then Laurie made a bold move.

She turned to Angela, placed one hand on her unbuttoned waistband, waved her other hand over her plate, palm down to signal her intentions, and uttered words that emanated from the depths of sincerity and purpose.

"I cannot eat anymore."

"What? What did she say, Marta?" Angelo asked, stifling Laurie's ploy to turn toward the one with whom she felt she had the better chance.

"*Lei non può mangiare di più. Ha mangiato abbastanza.* I have eaten enough, too, Angelo. Really, we cannot eat anymore. We had a late lunch. You've been generous enough already."

"You both will find room, *le mie cugine*. We haven't even had the main *course* yet. We'll take our time. You'll be fine."

"I don't know, Angelo. As I said, we had a pretty late lunch."

"Marty, I am serious," Laurie said. "I can't eat another thing. I am *dying* over here." Her cheeks were reddening then – either from shrimp toxicity or from her heart pumping harder than usual. Regardless of the impetus, within seconds her normally pale-to-olive-colored flesh had taken on an appearance of extreme asphyxiation. She announced that her pants zipper was continuing to slide open as we spoke, on its own will, and that none of us should be surprised if she stripped down to her underpants and allowed the flesh of her back thighs to adhere themselves to the plastic cushions.

"So, Marta," Angelo continued as if sound had not punched through either set of our lips, "how is your mother? She was such a sweet woman. Does she remember her visit with us? We certainly remember her. We had dinner at Maria's house, eh? She liked the *calamari* Maria served. We had that when you visited, didn't we? Maybe we should have *calamari* for the main meal. Do you like *calamari*, Marta, like your mother?"

"Yes, Angelo, I do. I love *calamari*. But…"

"How about Laura? Does she like *calamari*?"

"I think so, Angelo, but she is saying that she truly cannot eat one more thing. Not one more thing, Laura is saying."

"Ask her if she likes swordfish. They have a delicious swordfish here. The part they serve comes from the base near the tail – the best part. They do a nice job with the swordfish. Ask Laura if she likes swordfish."

The error of incalculable proportions was that we admitted we liked swordfish and *calamari*. If we had had the forethought to lie, we might have been better armed to avoid the main course. But in a delusional state, both of us signaled our fondness for each and, as a result, Angelo summoned the waiter to the table for more wine, more bread, more water, and dinner – *una pizza* for Angela, swordfish for Laura, and *calamari* for him and for me.

In the brief silence that followed again, I could not compel myself to think of one of the questions I had on reserve. The *pasta* and sea critters from the last round had settled into the uppermost regions of my stomach and had begun their climb up my esophagus toward the parts of the brain that control coherent language and a mood of intelligence.

Laurie backed herself away from the table. When she lifted her napkin from her lap, at a moment when Angela and Angelo were engaging in the Sicilian dialect with the owner, she debuted a zipper that was completely down to its base and some white underpants that could have served as a Jiffy Pop stand-in.

I raised my shirt in return, and the look of horror that spread across her face screamed of a distortion to which I was not privy. I could not see over my own self to review the scene at which she was balking. I did have the sense, though, that part of her concern was how her younger relative could have gone from a normal-looking specimen at the beginning of the trip to a woman who was primed to give birth to a second generation of Amazons at any moment.

The dialect continued between the three Sicilians, so Laurie and I were able to strategize as we watched each other scan the room for pockets of oxygen.

"What are we gonna do, Lau'?"

"We're gonna die right here."

"Should we fake an allergic episode?"

"We're gonna die right here."

"I am serious. What are we gonna do?"

"Die right here."

The laughter that followed sent lightning bolts of pain straight to our hearts, as if to remind us that this was not the least bit funny. We were strapped in a culinary black hole, a consumption nebula, and there was no room for hilarity.

We grew ever more grateful for every second that elapsed without another plate finding its way to our table. But then the inevitable happened. A parade of thin gentlemen, dressed in black pants, black belts, and starched shirts, carrying more wine, more bread, more water, and four large plates, appeared and were then followed by one more waiter carrying four salads.

One-by-one the items were placed in front of us. Angelo licked his lips, Angela raised her knife and fork to begin cutting her *pizza*, and the two of us remained cemented in our positions – upright but increasingly hunched.

"Eat," Angelo commanded.

"We will. We are just enjoying the aroma," I said, feeling quite buoyed by my delay tactics – until Angelo stretched across my body to cut portions from his cousins' dinners and raise those portions to our mouths.

"Laura! Marta! Eat. It's delicious."

Like gluttonous robots, we followed our orders and called on our powers of denial to repeat the action of chewing and of swallowing – all the while resisting, resisting, and wondering where it could possibly be going.

But then the unspeakable happened.

Laurie and I continued to eat.

For despite the mountains of food that had already been poured into our pie-holes that day, which back home would certainly have deadened the senses and limited the focus to quantity over quality, there was one absolute – the *calamari* were superb. The swordfish, from right near the base of the tail, was unparalleled.

I cut into my thin, tender *calamari*, that were accompanied only by a shallow bath of oils and spices to make them feel happier, with a reverence that bordered on obscene. Laurie allowed her pieces of swordfish to melt in her mouth and invited them down her throat by tilting her head back, with eyes closed, as she savored each flavor of the perfectly-prepared fish.

Angelo smiled.

And then, not long after we had begun, our plates were cleaned.

When the forks rested quietly on the porcelain surface, we inflated our cheeks again and blew out air from the depths of our *corps*.

Laurie stood to stretch, to shift position, while her completely unzipped pants did not move one centimeter. Her stomach, which traditionally compares more to an ironing board than a goiter, was thwarting the powers of one of the strongest forces known to humanity. Gravity.

I leaned back in my chair, unbuttoned the shorts that had been three sizes too big, and sloped down onto my cushion in a gesture that might have bordered on rude and inappropriate; but I calculated that death at the table would have been even more so.

Angelo had won each battle and was clearly winning the war. We had been forced to surrender, Laura and I, and our prisoner status had tossed us between the extremes of utopia and hell and utopia again.

In the silence following the latest round, I poked at my salad. "It's good for digestion," my mother used to say, quoting her father. And so I nibbled until only hints of olive oil and vinegar left a dainty film on an otherwise empty plate.

By the time dessert was proposed, we knew enough to order without resistance. In Italia, "no" means nothing when uttered at a dinner table. We were more inclined to preserve our oxygen for breathing more than for, say, speaking.

Earlier in the evening, we had relived Laurie's eloquent monologue at Il Latini when she praised the glories of *tiramisù*. Her *dolce*, therefore, was an inevitability. But then Angelo suggested we try *fichi d'india* – the prickly fruits that dangle from the cacti that graze on the Sicilian countryside.

"Have you seen these at home?"

"No," I answered then, but I had, in the fresh fruit section of our monolithic grocery stores. I barely recognized that they were related when I first saw them in Sicily. The American relatives of the Italian treasures were sickly and browning and had lost their external feistiness. And with each qualitative step away from the *fichi d'india* of Italy, the price of the *fichi d'india* of the United States grew exponentially until, back home, we were programmed to lay down *tanti dollari* for a piece of rotten fruit – fruit that grows gloriously within every turn on this island.

So, I had seen them, but I had never been inspired to eat them.

The waiter scurried away one last time with two kinds of desserts and a collection of drinks etched in his memory. Despite the spontaneous obesity that had swept over our table, we were looking forward to the *fichi d'india* and to Angelo sharing another nook of his pride.

When the waiter returned, he was carrying everything on a round tray, except for the *fichi d'india*. They were being escorted by the owner of the restaurant, who had been overcome with shock by our admission that neither of us had ever eaten that brand of delicacy. It was as if we had casually mentioned that television had not yet made it to the United States or that aqueducts brought all our city folk a fresh supply of water each morn.

The owner pulled up a chair at the head of the table with five *fichi* on a small dessert plate. Two were red, one was yellow/white, and two were green. Even those things that spring from the earth reflect the colors of the flag and honor the natives' unmatched patriotism.

We both reached to touch the *fichi*, oval-shaped fruits the size of small pears, but were abruptly brushed back by all the Sicilians.

"No!"

"*Attenzione*!"

"They are dangerous, *cugine*!"

With that, the owner carefully placed two of his fingers, already protected inside synthetic gloves, in-between the prickles of the fig and began to use a knife to remove the aggressive outer skin. He had barely begun the process when Angelo reached his arm across the front of my body, snapped his fingers, and asked for the plate of *fichi* to be passed from the owner to him. With reluctance, the owner gave in, and Laurie and I watched the hallowed fruit pass from the owner's possession into the hands of Angelo. It was his right, apparently, to introduce the *fichi* to his guests, especially guests who were family.

The ritual then began again, with Angelo placing his fingers in-between the prickles to continue to skin the harsh exterior, exposing a sweetness that was reminiscent of watermelon – cool to the taste and light. The *fichi* proved to be an unobtrusive cap to the meal, and they cleansed the palate and helped eradicate the dawdling flavors of the festival of food without adding a burden of poundage.

In a handful of minutes, our dessert dishes looked more emptied than filled – a vision that was in sharp contrast to at least *three* of us at the table. Still, we welcomed an *espresso* and a shot of Averna, tacitly rejoiced as nearly all of the remaining dishes were cleared, and then, mercifully, tarried at the table with a sense of peace – knowing that no more food was on its way.

If, I mused, we spend our minutes dancing across a spectrum between life and death, where at any given moment we tap closer to one end than the other, I knew that that night had pushed me closer to death, by culinary infusion, than ever before. But even so, so quickly after the last liquids surrounded the last tidbits of the evening's fare, I fondly reminisced about the *calamari* as if they were vanquished friends. And in the end, after all that had been swallowed that evening, I still yearned to pluck a morsel of a disarmed fig and toss an ounce of sweetness into my mouth.

....

The first lightning bolt and deafening thunder clap occurred within seconds of my having asked Angelo if his parents were buried above the ground in a mausoleum or in the ground in a simple coffin. His response was delivered with the same polite revulsion as his reaction to my having asked if Angela had a job.

"Pshtt" was the sound he pushed through his teeth and lips as he wagged his head from side-to-side. "Above the ground. We would *never* bury our relatives in the ground."

"It is different in the United States, Angelo. A lot of people are placed in the earth after death."

"Not here. Here that is considered brutal."

"Why?"

"It just isn't done," he said.

The conversation had run its course.

And in the aftermath of its closure, I knew that forays into cultural minefields forced anyone who was listening to reconsider the power of tradition. Why was the ground so disdainful to some, and how had that disdain gotten lost on its journey across the Atlantic? Was it spiritual – suggesting there was a divergence regarding our views of the body's path after death? Or was it merely a practicality, hinting that one culture was more focused on consumption of space and simplicity than the other?

Three long and sharpened lightning bolts crossed paths in the sky. In front of us, the view over the valleys and the waters from the stone wall in Altavilla Milicia offered a show of force and brilliance. Behind us, the church of the Black Madonna did the same as the crashing echoes of the lightning's wrath spread across the skies.

When I was young, *tuoni e lampi*, thunder and lightning, petrified me. It was inevitable. My mother's fear was transmitted to each of her children as she ushered us away from water pipes and electrical outlets and into windowless spaces with the first hint of a rumble – all the while running for our rubber-soled shoes, intended to rebuff the potency of a lightning strike. But in Sicilia, the four of us stood perched on the precipice of a cliff, with a stone guardrail in our hands to watch the show.

When sheets of rain started to slice into the comfort of our front-row seats, we remained. Angela wore the American baseball cap I had unhooked from my backpack and given her at dinner. Laurie and I pulled the hoods from our anoraks up over our heads. Angelo let the rivulets stream down his face without lifting one finger to wipe away the flood.

The lightning continued in parallel paths across the heavens. Thunder rocked the soul of the Earth, set off car alarms, and barely quieted before more lightning struck, illuminating the faces and bodies of four drenched and stuffed relatives living in the moment and sacrificing physical comforts for more lasting memories.

The car ride back to Palermo was filled with the energy of little children. Waves splashed up to and over the windows of Angelo's Fiat. Wrath and beauty continued to fly across the skies and down toward the ground. Swords of rain pierced the dirt and eroded the valleys, forcing mud-streams into our course.

I wondered about those buried below the ground.

When we pulled into the parking lot of their home, Angelo and Angela, from the front seat, beckoned us up to their apartment to prepare ourselves for bed. "No," we pressed, over the din of the downpour, "we should head back to our bed and breakfast in Pettineo. But thank you very, very much."

"No, no," they answered. "You *must* come up to our apartment, at least to wait until the storm lets up. But we think you should spend the night. We know these Sicilian storms – this will not let up for some time."

"Thank you both, really, thank you, but we should probably get back to our bed and breakfast. You know, they are expecting us. We are the only two guests there."

"Marta!" Angelo called out from the front seat as he twisted his body around, turned on the car light, and looked straight into my eyes. "What are you thinking? This weather is very dangerous. The drive back to Pettineo is curvy and hilly. You could get stuck between here and there. Even *I* wouldn't consider making that drive tonight. Two women traveling alone. I cannot let you go. I will not let you go. It is too dangerous."

An air of futility permeated the car – reminiscent of our resisting food at the restaurant. Still, we felt compelled to battle. We had paid for the bed and breakfast. Its setting was idyllic. We wanted to wake up to dogs barking across the valley and to olive branches outside our windows. We wanted to stroll into the kitchen, make *espresso*, and spread homemade marmalade on our fresh bread. We wanted to see Tusa one more time in the early-morning light.

But then Angelo did something.

He reached his arm over the front seat, gave me a tender tap alongside my right ear, grabbed my cheeks with the same hand, and said softly, "*Martuccia*, *Martuccia*, please, please stay. I am begging you. We have a nice extra bedroom. We will give you *caffè* and breakfast in the morning. Then you can get right on your way. Please. *Ti prego*."

As soon as he stopped speaking, I turned to Laurie, who had already begun reaching for the door handle. She had heard "*Martuccia*" and understood, in an instant, that another surrendering was inevitable. Before I could find the time to tell her that we should probably stay, she was out of the car, pulling up the hood to her anorak, and bending over so that I could see her smile.

"Come on, *Martuccia*," she said, "let's go. I'll carry your pack."

"*Grazie, cugina*."

"*Di niente, cugina*," she said in perfect Italian.

But it was far from nothing. I knew it was far from nothing.

Did you know that I can stick my tongue up my nose?" "No," my cousin Laurie winced. "I did not know that." Her ignorance of my talent was symbolic of something – symbolic of the fact that although we were relatives, we were also relative strangers. She didn't know a lot about me. I didn't know a lot about her.

Time does what time does, I thought that night, as I looked across the room at Laurie, curled up in a daybed that warmed her soaked flesh. Time did what time does. And in twelve lightning-quick days, her gesture in the car that night was also symbolic of something –

symbolic of something that no one outside our circle of twelve days would ever understand or appreciate, no matter how much we wanted them to or how much they wanted to.

"Can you hear the rain outside?" Laurie asked. "It's still coming down like mad. I'm glad we stayed. Not only because of the weather, but because of Angelo and Angela, too. I think we made them happy."

"Me, too. Me, too, *cugina*."

And then we closed our eyes and allowed the steady pelting of the rain to lull us to sleep.

Chapter Eleven

THE PRESENT
Italia/Gli Stati Uniti

The sky had orchestrated a dramatic clearing when we awoke the next morning. Bright blues and puffy whites had replaced the chorus of the evening before and shed some light on the soundness of our having stayed – as plants lay spent in Palermitano window boxes, and deep puddles rested on cobblestone alleys.

Angela and Angelo were dressed and waiting for us in the kitchen when we emerged from our bedroom and morning ablutions. *Espresso* had awakened us earlier, having bubbled slowly on the gas stove and sent its aura down the hall and into our sleep. Only *caffè* and the ubiquitous melba crackers were resting on their countertop when we entered. For the first time, we were grateful for the modest manner in which Italians eat in the new day.

The tiny kitchen table had room for only Laurie and me, so Angela and Angelo stood in their fine clothing and humored us by answering our questions about the proper way to make *espresso* in one of those silver percolators. A recap of the previous evening's meal followed as did a summary of our immediate future – a trip back to Pettineo and a few dwindling days as tourists before our flight home.

"Why don't you both come to America sometime?," I asked. "Especially now that you're retiring soon, Angelo."

"We don't like to fly," they said in unison. "When we travel, we travel only by train."

"How about a ship?"

"Now that's something to think about. Maybe a ship." And then they looked at each other, giving a halfhearted nod.

I knew I would never see them in the United States.

Their island, and sometimes their mainland, and less frequently the continent that is attached, keep them where they want to be.

The four of us walked to our car *in silenzio*. Our sandals and toes were moistened by the aftermath of Nature's fury.

"Please come back," Angela said when we reached the Daewoo, holding onto my hand. "Please come back and visit us."

"Oh, we will, Angela. We love it here. Sicily will always pull us back." And then she smiled the kind of smile that led her in-between two places – knowing precisely why we felt the way we did and wondering just how it is that their home casts such a spell.

"Please be careful," Angelo implored as we threw our packs into the car. "And let us know when you get back to Pettineo. We expect to hear from you."

"*Va bene*, *cugino*. We will call when we return."

And then we all fell into the depths of one another's embraces – embraces that were enhanced by the kisses that could be heard echoing off the walls of the courtyard.

"Thank you, Angelo and Angela. Thank you for everything."

"Pshtt. It was nothing," they said, synchronized once more. "You are family. It is what families do."

And then his hand reached up and touched our cheeks – first Laurie's and then mine – until it left our faces to reach for the hand of his wife. And it was in that position that we left them, two hands holding, two hands waving, as we pulled back onto the capital streets, leaving the gaze of our relatives only to stare into the eyes of those big-city strangers, feeling nothing but calm and protection.

The last few days of our trip were like riding the last few feet of a roller coaster. We knew it was coming to an end, and what had already happened had to be far more exhilarating than what was to come. That was inevitable – for the last few days returned us to a tourist status, out from under the arms of relatives.

We picnicked with *mortadella* on bread, grapes, and Parmesan cheese in Santo Stéfano di Camastra, along a terrace with the city's ceramics decorating every turn. Good-byes were offered to Teresa and her husband, and we hoped that a return to Pettineo would find her there. We wended our way through the hills and valleys of Sicily on our way to Taormina, allotting two hours of travel for what consumed six hours of time. We screamed out "*fichi d'india*" whenever we spotted one growing on the sides of our narrow path, or whenever the spirit moved us, and then would lapse into episodes of laughter, with Laurie pounding the wheel of the car and me unbuttoning my pants and wiping tears from my eyes.

We missed our train from Taormina to Rome, and a local taxi driver, with eyes that were pools of sparkling blue, said he would *not* take us up into the city to find a hotel – but later changed his mind when we lost ourselves in stories of his culture.

Our hotel featured a view of Mt. Etna as well as the busiest wallpaper known to humanity, spread wildly on every speck of plaster that surrounded our beds. Dinner had us seated next to a boundless, deafening Pomposity Master, who viewed her command of Italian as brilliant despite her pronunciation, which combined the most enervating elements of Julia Child with Queen Elizabeth.

Our departure from the Taormina *stazione* the next day, after a serenade of *O sole mio* by Giuseppe, a lifetime officer of the station, led us to a train, that climbed onto a ship, that got us across the Strait of Messina, and back to the mainland of Italy. We were moved north to Rome where we focused on St. Peter's Cathedral, the *Pietà*, the Vatican Museums, the Sistine Chapel, and *The Last Judgment*.

Laurie and I climbed to the top of the dome, over a variety of slanted steps, and looked upon the splendor of Rome under the apostles who stand watch near its highest point.

I was aware that we were growing quieter with each passing hour. Laurie's mind was halfway between Rome and home. My mind was still firmly locked in Italy.

Even when I *am* home, my mind remains locked in Italy.

On our last night, with the two of us in our pajamas and our luggage nearly fully-packed and resting at the end of our beds, Laurie asked me for a translation.

"I want to be able to say something in perfect Italian when people back home ask me about the trip," she said.

"What would you like to say?"

"This trip was the best trip of my life."

"*Questa vacanza è stata la più bella vacanza della mia vita.*"

"*Questa vacanza...*" she began, "Will you write it down for me? Phonetically? So that I can memorize it?"

"It *was* pretty amazing, wasn't it Lau'?"

"Magic. Magic. I'm telling you, we had angels. I can't wait to tell people about it."

"I'm not sure that will turn out the way you think it will."

"What do you mean?"

"People don't understand, Lau'. They won't understand. Some will try hard. Ask a lot of questions. Look at the photos. Listen to the stories. And others, amazingly, won't do *any* of that. But even those who try will fall short. They'll have to.

"Seeing pictures of *nonna's* baptismal font and *nonno's* birth certificate," I continued, "is not the same as touching them. Telling people that the first word we heard Iolanda speak was 'Rubeo' will not be the same as if they had heard it for themselves. Repeating my version of what it felt like to have Angelo's hands on my cheeks and having him call me '*Martuccia*' ..."

"I think people *will* understand."

"I hope you're right. I truly hope you're right."

On a classic fall day in late-October, just one week after Laurie and I had returned home, I packed up my photographs from Italy, printed out a fresh copy of our blossoming family tree, got in my car, and drove to the home of my then eighty-one year-old mother.

We sat next to each other on her soft couch and sipped tea as we leafed through each photograph.

"Who are they again?" she would ask. "My second cousins?"

"Yes, Mum. Pasquale's and Iolanda's *nonna* and your mother's father were sister and brother."

"And this is my mother's baptismal font?"

"Yes, this is the font where your mother was baptized. In *La Chiesa di Sant'Eustachio* in Campo di Giove."

My mother reached her hands up to her forehead then and shook her head from side-to-side and started to cry.

"Mom was baptized right there?"

"Yes. Right there. And we saw her birth certificate and the home where she was born, and we uncovered the name of the witness to her birth. Antonetti Francesco. Do you believe it?"

"Antonetti Francesco? Like my name?"

"Like your name. And we have a photo of your father's birth certificate, and…"

"And who are they again, dear?" she would ask as she pointed to the family photograph from Campo di Giove.

"They are Pasquale and Iolanda. Their grandmother and your grandfather were sister and brother."

The afternoon hours spilled away in just that fashion – with us sipping tea and handling each photograph and yearning to share histories the other did not know. And with me watching my mother's wrinkled fingers move from one level to the next on a family tree that was branching out in the warmth of an uncovered history, and the warmth of a mother's heart – a heart that had lived through some of the events that a family tree portrays with such brevity.

When we were finished, my mother moved herself up off of the couch and into her bedroom. I waited quietly, until she called me inside – to face her as she stood small, and tall, in front of her mahogany dresser.

Before she spoke, she looked straight up into my eyes, and I looked into hers. And she raised her right hand to my left cheek – so that I would stand closer to the face of my future.

"Put out your hand, dear," she said when she finally spoke.

And so I did.

And on it she placed a simple, fragile ring.

Softened from its age. Softened from its years of loyalty.

I lifted up the band from my palm, between thumb and finger, and carried it toward the sun, squinting to examine its character and the tattered details of its inscription.

"It reads 'AR to BR – 1913.'"

"Yes, honey. This is the wedding ring of my parents. Antonio Ragonese to Beatrice Rubeo." And with that, my mother's familiar fingers, worn, seasoned, strong, invited me to slip the band onto the ring finger of my right hand. And then she said, "I cannot think of another person I would rather give this to. Another person who'd appreciate it more."

And there we stood.

In silence.

Soaking in the splendor of the fleeting present, as birth certificates and aging façades and distant family lived vividly inside the borders of that tiny ring.

And then I found the breath to speak, to ask my mum if she were certain that just now, just then, was the time to pass along a greatest treasure. And if I were truly the one to whom it should be passed.

"I've never been more sure, *Martuccia*," is how she answered. "And now is the time. Now is always the time."

And then my mother and I embraced.

My arms reached around her shrinking frame, and she nestled her head just under my own as I hugged her and patted her back in gentle rhythms. In time she looked up, and her comforting cheeks met mine. And I felt her arms and those hands, those mother's hands, return the soothing taps. And I started to sob.

For our afternoon of tea.

For the ring on my finger.

For bridges built.

For a present she understood.
And a past she no longer remembers.
And a day I know I never will forget.

Alla storia, I whispered, into my mother's ear.
Alle radici.
Alla famiglia.
To history. To roots. To family.
To all that is lasting.
To all that is real.

And then my mother's fingers lifted my hand, and their ring, her ring, my ring, toward the sun. And we watched as a ray shone down upon the circle – to highlight an eternal path, a familial path, of truth.

- *Fine* -

Photograph – The 1913 Wedding of Antonio Ragonese and Beatrice Rubeo

THE EPILOGUE

In the summer of 2001, Campo di Giove welcomed me back with a love and generosity I had come to expect, and that time its reach extended around my cousin Michael, the brother of Laura, and his wife Suzanne. I trust it was the passion of Laura's and my adventure that propelled more family into the grasp of Italy and to the cousins who live happily and peacefully in the mountains of Abruzzo.

In returning, I was allowed to taste, again, the discoveries of old in Campo di Giove – the baptismal font, the birth certificate, and the ancestral home. And I was led down other paths, as yet uncharted by those from "the other side" – as we met more relatives, Francesco, Vitantonio, and Giuseppe, the brother, husband, and son of Lina, respectively. And we were invited into our *nonna's* birth home by the owner, who happened to stroll by as we were struggling to see into the remnants of our grandmother's life.

But most of all, returning allowed me to swim in the waves of my Italian cousins' love while they showered us with the warmth of family and the pride of their tiny village – as they fed us the freshest of meats, unparalleled roasted potatoes, utopian peas, breads, *dolci*, *gelato*, and, of course, the *mozzarella* of the gods, all of which was bathed in homemade wine and after-dinner liqueurs.

When it came time to part, Michael turned to me to ask that I translate what was living inside his heart. His cheeks grew pale as he began, and his face was wearing the look that precedes the kind of honesty that waits to emerge from its home deep under our flesh.

"Please tell them that it was a privilege to have met them." And then he paused before he continued, "And please tell them that it is an honor to be a part of their family."

Iolanda, Giuseppe, Pasquale, Marta, Filomena, Angelo, Serena, Lina, Vitantonio (l-r)

I moved through the translation with difficulty, because the emotions of my American cousin were augmented with tears of my own. Still, *la famiglia italiana* listed intently as each word spilled from my lips and met their ears. And then they reacted, with arms around our bodies and kisses from cheek-to-cheek.

When my cousin Lina and I left the comfort of our embrace, I placed my hands on her cheeks and quivered through the Italian to tell her what was clear to me right then. That after two visits, after two short visits, she was like a dear friend to me then.

Lina reached her hands up through my arms and placed them on my cheeks and responded with what was clear to her. "*No, Marta, no*," in an Italian tone that was graced with class and clarity and sweetness. "*Tu mi sei come una sorella.*"

No, Marta, no. You are like a *sister* to me.

We pulled closer to each other then and could not help but wonder how all of our boundaries could feel so free to come tumbling down as we skirted the years such closeness often requires.

Our tears remained with us as we left the relatives and headed down the winding streets away from Campo di Giove. We were satiated with the love and nurturing of a family we were delighted to call our own. And while our emotional sides lived in the purity of the moment, our analytical sides tried to understand the depth and the sincerity of what we felt. What I know is that my past makes me young again and brings back to life all that was simple, all that was unedited, and all those who had been there to make it that way.

I return to Italy to connect with a past that helped shape me...
but that runs the risk of being forgotten...
unless I keep it alive.

After some time, when the warmth of Campo di Giove had to strive harder to offset the coolness of our new anonymity, I came to ask my cousin's wife, Suzanne, what this might have possibly meant to her. She was, after all, linked only by marriage. Not by blood.

Her initial silence seemed to fill the car – until she found the energy to push her thoughts through the weight of her own very real and very deep tears.

When she spoke, her words were simple, yet powerful.

"I just think you are so lucky. So lucky...."

And I nodded.

And Mike nodded.

And we wished that we were headed back up that mountain.

And into the arms of our youth.

ACKNOWLEDGMENTS

Campo di Giove, Italia

To my relatives in Campo di Giove, Pasquale, Iolanda, Adelina, Filomena, Angelo, Lina, Serena, and then Francesco, Vitantonio, and Giuseppe, I thank you for welcoming me to the birthplace of my grandmother and for helping me uncover what might have gotten lost in our family's history. Thank you for bridging the gap that an ocean expanse and 100 years had created and for welcoming me into your home for conversation, food, sleep, and unconditional love, as if we had known one another forever.

To the Campo di Giove town hall employees, Nello and Tonino, I am indebted to you for your patience and for sharing my excitement as we uncovered the documents detailing my family's names, births, home, and occupations.

Tusa, Italia

To Angelo and Angela, thank you for welcoming me back to Sicily one more time and for treating me to a most exquisite meal of seafood on the shores of your beautiful island. Thank you, too, for your foresight and kindness in offering me a restful place to sleep to avoid the wrath of the Sicilian skies. I am forever heartened and struck by your unabashed acceptance of and generosity toward your distant family.

To the Tusan town hall employees, Anna, Pina, and Santina, your commitment to my dream was extraordinary and filled with a calm determination. I am so grateful you did not allow the early roadblocks to dissuade you from finding the documents of my history.

Gli Stati Uniti/The United States

To Adolfo Caso of Branden Books, thank you, again, for allowing me to bring my love of Italy, and my roots, to life for others to share.

To my sister, Cindy Cummings Neprash, and her husband, Brian Neprash, much gratitude to you both for your generosity and for providing such a peaceful setting as I worked on the final draft of my book. Thanks, too, for the laughter – the daily laughter – that *greatly* enhanced my nomadic summer.

To Lysa Rowe, thank you for following up on my résumé and for opening up a path for me that allows me to work with students *and* to write. To the parents of the students I tutor, thank you for the inordinate endorsement you have given me over the years and for entrusting me with the standards and visions for your children. And to the wonderful array of students I tutor, many thanks for the beams of intelligence, kindness, determination, and humor I see in each of you and for the progress you make when all of those qualities come together.

To the readers of the early draft, Mary Ward Burns, Posy Dana, Mary E. Dolbear, Sarah Klett, Laurie Ragonese, and Suzanne Fahey Ragonese, thank you very much for your extreme commitment of time and energy.

To Gail Mardfin of PLP Graphic Design Services, thank you for transforming the cover and photographs to publishable form as you brought your expertise to bear. Thank you to photographer David F. Saul for allowing a second glimpse of the author snapshot and to Jahdeam Dempsey for helping me with the scanning of photographs in the early stages. To Fernanda Conley, thank you for helping me to perfect the translations between English and Italian. To Ellen Slade, thank you for walking Jesse and Jackson after my ligament tear in my knee. Clearing my head of canine-guilt allowed me to write more freely. Thanks to Missy, at Maine's Cedar Haven Campgrounds, for the restful space in which I considered the last phases of editing.

To Laurie Ragonese, *mia cugina*, thank you for our exceptional, shared journey to Italy. It is always a remarkable trip, as you learned within the first day of our arrival, but it is particularly remarkable when it is made with relatives, whose histories and desires often intersect in innumerable ways. I am grateful for those intersections and for the unparalleled degrees to which our eyes and hearts have been opened. *Fichi d'india per sempre*!

Finally, to my family and friends, thank you for your love, support, interest, and enthusiasm each time I live, figuratively or literally, in the land, the history, the people, and the roots that make me feel free.

And to my mother, my dear, sweet mother – I dedicate this book to you, Mum, so that you will know, undeniably and forever, that I am eternally indebted to you for so much of who I am, so much of what I hold important, and so much of what is good in me. *Ti voglio bene, mamma – angelo mio.*

Alla famiglia. Sempre alla famiglia!

PHOTOGRAPHY CREDITS

Photograph	Year Taken	Page	Photographer
Nonno's/Nonna's Wedding	1913	Front	Unknown Source
Nonna/Her Granddaughter	1961	Back	Unknown Source
Nonno's Birth Certificate	1999	Back	Laura M. Ragonese
Antoinette F. Cummings	2000	5	Martha T. Cummings
Italian Map	NA	8	Microsoft Clip Art
Nonna/Her Granddaughter	1961	24	Unknown Source
Nonna's Baptismal Font	2001	41	Michael A. Ragonese
Tuscan Cypress Trees	1986	108	Martha T. Cummings
Tuscan Grapes	1994	112	Martha T. Cummings
Sicilian Urn	1999	118	Laura M. Ragonese
Nonno/His Grandchildren*	1954	150	Joseph F. Cummings, Jr.
Nonno's Sicilian Façade	1999	152	Martha T. Cummings
Nonno's Birth Certificate	1999	156	Laura M. Ragonese
Nonna/Her Children	1961	170	Unknown Source
Cousins Laura/Marta	1999	193	A Roman Tourist
Nonno's/Nonna's Wedding	1913	197	Unknown Source
Abruzzese Family/Marta	2001	200	Michael A. Ragonese
Author	1997	207	David F. Saul

* Pictured in the photograph (l-r): Cynthia Cummings, Antonio Ragonese, Laura Ragonese, Marcia Ragonese, Anthony Cummings, Joseph Cummings III

ABOUT THE AUTHOR

Martha T. Cummings was raised in Southborough, Massachusetts, a small town several miles west of Boston, and attended public schools in that area. In 1980, after earning an anthropology degree from Bryn Mawr College, she began a teaching career. After five years in education, Cummings moved to Perugia, Italy, home to a university for foreigners, to learn Italian to be able to meet and converse with her relatives in Abruzzo and Sicily. Her first book, *Straddling The Borders – The Year I Grew Up in Italy*, chronicles that experience. Cummings reentered the educational field following her time in Perugia, but ultimately left teaching to pursue her writing interests.

She now lives along the Rhode Island coast with her two dogs, Jesse (a Brittany) and Jackson (a Beagle), and divides her time between being an author and a tutor. Much of the time she is not writing or soaking up the beauty of life by the ocean, she is dreaming of ways to return to her primary passion – Italy.